BEEN THERE, DONE THAT, GOT THE GILET

A spectators guide to the Tour de France

JAN BOARDMAN

AuthorHouse™ UK
1663 Liberty Drive
Bloomington, IN 47403 USA
www.authorhouse.co.uk
UK TFN: 0800 0148641 (Toll Free inside the UK)
UK Local: 02036 956322 (+44 20 3695 6322 from outside the UK)

This book is printed on acid-free paper.

ISBN: 979-8-8230-8785-8 (sc)
ISBN: 979-8-8230-8786-5 (e)

Library of Congress Control Number: 2024910621

Print information available on the last page.

Published by AuthorHouse 05/30/2024

authorHOUSE®

Introduction

How much do you know about Cycling? Can you name a cycling Road Race? No matter what you answer to the first question, the answer to the second is probably going to be the Tour de France. It's a race with 22 teams of eight riders that chase each other round France for 3 weeks. It is actually so much more than that though.

If you have watched the race on TV at any time then you will have experienced about 10% of what the tour offers. On TV you get to see the race itself but you miss so much more that can only be experienced by going to France and watching for yourself.

For me the Tour is about meeting people, from all over the world. It's about France and visiting all the places that you would never think of going to. It's about the racing, the speed, the noise, the power, the exertion, the fluid dynamics of the peleton. It's about fun as the entire route is one giant 3,500 kilometre party! It's about logistics and the scale of the infrastructure behind the Tour. It's about challenging yourself to do something you have never considered doing before which I totally surprised myself with!

Over 9 Tours I have seen something of 129 stages, 13 rest days, 2 stages of La Course, and 7 stages of the Tour de France Femmes. Every stage has been different. Every stage has had something new to experience. I have selected some of these stages that enable me to show something different each time, which I hope will help anyone who wants to experience the Tour themselves to work out what is possible where and how to get the most out of your visit. Everyone should experience the Tour at least once as it's Awesome!

I have split up this book into sections as this is the easiest way to help you decide what you might want to see and then decide how to do it.

1 – Mountains – Summit finishes or mid stage mountians, both are worth a visit

2 – Starts – So much happens here that they are definitely worth a visit

3 – Sprint finishes – Not my favourite for many reasons

4 – Time trials – I love a time trial, team or individual.

5 – Cobbles – Painful but such fun

6 – Rest days – Not at all restful

7 – Downhills - Scary

8 – Hilly Stages – Varied with so many options of what to see

9 – How lucky am I days! – OMG!

10 – Intermediate Sprint Points – These are usually fun and can fill a transfer type day very well

11 – Miscellaneous – No categorie to put these days in.

12 – Planning – So Important to get the most out of any visit to the tour.

I am not a photographer, and the photos added after each chapter were taken on my phone! They are at least in focus (mostly!) but they are not very high resolution. I have only added 20 of the 10,000+ that I have so I hope you can still enjoy them.

Mountains.

There are distinct types of mountains, and places to watch them from at the Tour. I have done most of them at some point or another over the last 9 years. They are divided into categories or levels of difficulty for the riders - 4 (even I can get up these ok!), 3, 2, 1, and finally Hors Categorie HC (Oh my God!)

There will be differences between a mid-stage mountain and one that is a summit finish for access, fun, what you see, etc. It is also fun to watch the riders go downhill if you want to scare yourself silly!

How do you get where you need to be? One thing to be aware of is that the roads will close early morning or even the day before towards the base of any cat one or HC climb, whether it is a mid-stage or a summit finish. Frequently, the closest you will get with a car is around 6 kilometres. If you are in a Campervan hoping to park on the side of the mountain, then be aware the road could close 2 or 3 days before. Or even 2 weeks before for Mont Ventoux! If you do manage to get parked on the race route on the mountain, then if you have any part of your vehicle over the road, the police in 2022 started coming round the day before and moving people off the mountain!

Trains are possible and a good plan if there is one. Buses will be a problem as there are roads closures to contend with.

If you are planning to go to the climb and walk, then be aware that you will possibly have up to 6 kilometres to walk to the base of the climb, then at least a 10 kilometres walk up to watch the race come passed at the top, followed by walking all the way back down again! That is a walk of 32 kilometres and maybe more!! Or 5 or 6 hours! That is why I take my bike in my car. Even if I walk the 10 kilometres up the mountain, I can still ride the remaining 22 kilometres which is an enormous difference.

I will start with the first mountain I ever attempted. The category 1 Col d'Aspin. It was the final mountain of the days stage with a short downhill from the summit to the finish.

Friday, 8th July 2016. Col d'Aspin.

I am in the Pyrenees with a bike and wearing lycra. No one looks good wearing Lycra! I look worse than most as I am old, overweight and a bit self-conscious if I am honest. At least there were loads of other people wearing Lycra, so we all looked as bad as each other! It is stage 7 of this year's Tour de France and I intend to see some of it today. My plan (I always have a plan even if I do not always stick to it) was to park under a tree near Arreau, get my bike out of the car and then cycle hopefully 2 kilometres up the Category 1 mountain, the Col d'Aspin. Then watch the riders come past.

You might think this was a small challenge, but it was not for me! I only bought my first bike, since I did a paper round 50 years ago, 3 months before I arrived at the foot of the Col d'Aspin. Also, learning to ride a bike again, I had promptly fallen off and torn my thigh muscle! I had only got back on my bike 2 weeks before I left for France. I had only ever ridden on flat ground, no hills at all, meaning mountains were a complete unknown. Hence, no training, no bike handling skills, no fitness, too much weight and no expectations.

Part 1 of the plan was perfect. I had found a place to stay for the two nights either side of the stage, about 50 minutes from the foot of the climb. I drove from the Autoroute to as near to Arreau as I could get before the road closed. I found a huge tree to park under near a quarry on a large grass verge. The tree shade was essential as it was 25 degrees already at only 8.30 am. I was by no means the first car there, but I was glad I was early. I had driven passed hundreds of cyclists who were able to cycle the 25 kilometres from Lannemezan which even on flat roads was beyond me!

Part 2 was to get to the foot of the climb which meant cycling 5 kilometres along the valley and then through the centre of Arreau. What a lovely place. It is relatively flat for the Pyrenees, following the valley of a reasonable sized stream with old buildings made of stone everywhere. There were already cyclists and walkers going the same way as me. No chance of getting lost and as the roads by then were closed, it was an enjoyable way to ride my bike for the first time in France.

Part 3 – cycle a bit of the way up the climb. That was a shock! The road turned right at the foot of the climb, then went straight up hill and I only managed to get to the first bend before I had to stop. Must have managed 100 metres. Oh well, I could always watch the race from here. I sat down on a small wall, had a drink of water, and looked around me. There is a Eurosport car stopped right in front of me. Is that Greg Lemond? Yes, it is! Wow. I know I have spoken to him before, but I think I must have had a rush of blood to the head from the exertion of cycling this far as I go straight over to him and say hi! And he answers! We even have a short chat. I told him we had spoken before, but he will not remember that! I do not do selfies as I ruin the picture by just by being in it, but I did take a picture of him just to prove he is there.

He cycles off with the cameras rolling and I think to myself, this is not a good place from which to watch the race. As I can only see a short stretch of road, and I am feeling recovered and energised from meeting Greg, I decide I am going to cycle up the road a bit further. It was slightly easier after that first sharp start, and I manage to keep cycling for at least 5 minutes! I stopped for a drink and a rest, then actually set off again. Rinse and repeat 3 or 4 more times, and I came out of the trees to the most amazing views. It was so beautiful. The mountains towered all around me with jagged pointy tops, and I could see the road snaking up ahead of me. Looking back and wow! Arreau was visible below me. Way below me! I had no idea how high I had cycled up and I felt amazing.

The road was packed with people cycling and walking up that mountain. Many of them called out to see if I was ok sat there like a gnome on a wooden guardrail! Everyone was encouraging everyone else to keep going so I joined them and set off again. Another 5 minutes ride, rest, drink, and 5 minutes ride. I could now see a giant Polka Dot "T-Shirt" pegged out in a field just up in front of me, so I aimed for that. It looked like a wonderful place to watch the race come past. After another hour of riding and resting I made it! I had a chat with a lady from Wales who had set up camp there with a huge Welsh flag tied to a tree and a camping chair to sit on. It was so nice just chatting for about 20 minutes about cycling, France, riders, what we hoped to see etc. Arreau looked small and so far away now. No idea how far I had cycled but it must have been many kilometres! It was about five which was a result!

It is still early, 11 am, and the race was not due to come past until 5 pm ish. I had been cycling, resting, and chatting my way uphill for over 2 hours! I could see the road up ahead (but not the summit of the climb) and it looked to be relatively evenly up rather than steeply up. I ate some food, drank some more water, and thought – why not give it a go to the hairpin bends I could see which would have a great view of the race when it came past. I set off again on my stop start cycle ride and the views were fabulous. There was also some high cloud cover, so the temperature was still around the 25 degrees mark which was manageable. What seemed like hours later, I came to a sign that said 4 kilometres to the top! 4 Kilometres! OK, I am going to do this. I am going to aim for the top! Another rest, a chat with some people in Team sky shirts (they were Spanish!), some food and off I go again.

2 Kilometres to go sign! 1 kilometre to go sign. I can see the top! I can do this. Just keep pedalling, just keep pedalling. The clouds broke, the sun came out and the temperature rocketed up to well over 30 degrees. It is so hot now. 300 metres to go and I overheated. Big time. I had two bottles of water left and poured half of one over my head. I had my trusty Brolly with me as a sunshade, but I was forced to walk the final 300 metres. But I was at the top! I was at the TOP! There is no way I can describe my feelings at that moment. I had cycled (mostly) straight up for 12 kilometres at an average gradient of 6.6%, 800 metres of elevation gained going up to 1500 metres above sea level. The sense of achievement was off the chart. I was so proud of myself. I am still old, I am dreadfully unfit, I still look ridiculous

in Lycra, but I was at the top of a category 1 mountain in the Pyrenees! I took a couple of pictures of my bike against the barriers under the King of the Mountain (KOM) banner just to prove I had made it.

There was what looked like an entire village of tents and stalls over the fields to the sides of the KOM banner, selling tour related memorabilia, food, and drink, and even a place for bike repairs! Loads of people were camped up there as well. I had no idea this was all here as on the TV all you really get to see is the riders crossing the summit line, and then it is off to the adverts as soon as all the leaders are past. The organization of carting this all round France and depositing it on top of mountains each day is mind blowing. Build it the night before, take it down as soon as the race passes and then put it all back up overnight somewhere else! Every day for 21 days!

I locked my bike up and had a quick wander around the tent "village" and took some more photos of the view back down towards Arreau. It was just a speck in the distance in the valley below. I could even look down on the giant Polka Dot T Shirt way below me in the field.

What now? I could watch the race come past here but there were hundreds of people all over the top of the mountain with streams of others still coming up from both sides of the Col, so seeing much from here could be a problem. I thought the best plan would be to go back down the road to the Hairpin bends I had seen before as the view of the race from there would be special. On to the bike, roll off downhill and grab the brakes for dear life! I was terrified! The speed was too much for my riding ability and I tiptoed downhill with the brakes full on all the way to the hairpins! I have never been so scared in my life. Loads of other riders whizzed past me going much faster than I was, but they were obviously just nuts!

I stopped on a large grass verge above the highest hairpin and had a fabulous view in front of me going uphill for about 30 metres, but also below me down a long, straight road heading to the hairpins and all the way back to the T Shirt! It was about 2 pm by then so I set up camp – large very lightweight picnic mat that folded up into the size of a pack of cards, umbrella for shade, rucksack for a pillow, food, and drink - and promptly fell asleep! What a day!

After my short nap, I just lay there listening to all the people still coming up the mountain. I tried working out where they all came from just by listening to them. There were obviously French people, but also Spanish, Italians, Columbians (they speak Spanish differently), from the low countries, Belgium, and Holland, from the US and loads of Brits! I even spoke to a couple from South Africa! Other groups of people settled with me on the grass verge as well. It turned into a bit of a party. There were three young girls from Japan who were fun. An extended French family of about twenty also set up nearby with massive flags which they draped all over the rocky side of the road.

There was still a steady stream of people walking and cycling up towards the summit. There were Kids doing this! 9, 10 years old in full kit just cycling up and up this mountain! And I even saw a man with a kid's bike attached on the back of his carbon fibre road bike that had this lovely little girl on it trying to pedal as well! She must have been about five! All shapes and sizes try this! Everyone is so supportive and helpful. Whatever your cycling ability or fitness, just try it!

At 3 pm ish the Caravan turned up. I had seen this before as it travels the entire length of the route around 2 hours before the race comes past. It really is fun! However, halfway up a mountain it is still fun but the focus for me changes. On a stage where there are no hills and when I have walked a short distance to the race route, it great to get as much of the tat that is thrown from the floats as possible. Up a mountain on a bike that needs to be cycled back down 7 or 8 kilometres, it is better to try and avoid most of it. There is a lot, and it gets heavy and bulky to carry back down the road! I got a couple of cartons of Orange Juice and a bottle of water from the Vittel float which are always handy. Also, 5 or 6 Madelene's! Small cakes which are surprisingly tasty! I managed to get two packets of Haribo's which are obviously essential, but also some washing liquid, a few carrier bags, multiple key rings, several caps and hats, all sorts of stuff that had to be packed into my small ruck sack and carted off the mountain! I tried hiding under my Brolly to limit the amount of stuff thrown towards me but that was only partially successful.

Eventually the race came past with Steve Cummings in the lead chased by Vincenzo Nibali! I like to just point and press with my camera as the race comes past as I want to watch rather than view on a camera screen. I might as well stay at home and watch on TV doing that. I got some actual pictures of riders this time though! And some terrible ones but hey ho! I could see them coming in bits and pieces for miles! I got a bit excited shouting and cheering the riders on! I may even have jumped up and down!! I loved every minute of it.

One of the Cannondale riders threw his Bidon (Bottle) at my feet which was still quite full of an Isotonic drink so naturally I drank that and kept the bottle! When Ian Stannard came past, I said something to him, and he gave me a great smile which I caught right in the middle of a photo! The riders kept coming past for about 20 minutes. Even the Sprinters were going faster than I expected! When I think of the speed I went up that bit of the climb, it makes you realise just what these guys can do! And you are so close to them as they either race past really fast (GC and climbers) or struggle past still going a quite a speed (larger sprinters and classics men) or just make it look so easy as they chat and laugh their way to the top (the mountain domestiques and climbers who are not looking to win overall) and finally the injured or sick who still manage to get up that mountain fast! You know when the last rider has past you as there is the broom wagon bringing up the rear to sweep up any rider who just cannot go on. It even has a witch's broom attached to the front! It was empty today.

All that was left to do now was to cycle slowly back down the rest of the mountain to my car with all the other riders and walkers going back down the hill which made it extremely easy even if my hands hurt by the bottom. Grabbed the brakes hard all the way down!

My car was not too hot under the tree so all that was left to do was to drive back to the small B&B I was staying at and write up my daily report for my kids. They like to know I am still ok, but I bet they never expected me to do what I had!! I had cycled up a mountain, slept on a grass verge, spoken to loads of people from all over the world, been part of a massive party, and watched a bike race come past. What a fabulous way to spend a day.

Friday 8th July 2022. La Super Planches des Belle Filles.

I have been to this climb before! I did it in 2017 with my bike, and in 2019 in a Helicopter (that is a whole other story though!) This year I am riding again (pushing my bike realistically!). I stayed about 20 kilometres from where I knew I would want to leave my car. I tend to try and stay for a minimum of 2 nights in every place, so I do not get too tired. This time my planning meant I saw the start in Binche, in Belgium, then drove to Belfort on the 7th. I would then have the whole of the 8th to attack the mountain staying in the same place that night. I would then drive to the start in Dole on the 9th en route to the Alps.

I stayed in a lovely B&B just outside Belfort last night. It was quite remote with no shops, restaurants, or anything at all really! I had bought food in Binche before leaving as I knew that I would not manage to get anything when I finally arrived. France closes early! If you need food to eat in the evening and you are expecting to arrive after 6 pm, buy food in any supermarket, as early as you can. Good job I did too as I am sure I hit every set of roadworks in the whole of France! Instead of the expected 5 hour drive, it took nearer 8 hours!

The village was very pretty. The house was set right on the edge of the village overlooking a huge open field. The host had water for me to take from their fridge, and a cold beer if I wanted one which I most certainly did! The property had an excellent kitchen, a coffee machine, a sitting room, and a dining table set out on the patio looking across the fields. Lovely place and I was the only one there! There was a church nearby though. How do I know this? The bells rang every hour all night!!! With the heat, I had no choice but to leave the windows open, so my sleep was at best, disturbed!

Breakfast was included in the price, and it was amazing! There was fresh fruit salad using fruit from his own garden! He had also made a sort of rhubarb and berry tart which was great. There was the usual selection of bread related products but all so fresh. And Senseo coffee! No eggs today though but otherwise an excellent breakfast! In fact, there was so much, I made up two sandwiches for lunch with the bread and cheese and took half the Rhubarb and berry tart as well! I added orange juice to my water bottles as warm water tastes dreadful. The juice makes it easier to drink halfway up a mountain. I had left the bottles in the freezer overnight so I had at least the hope they might stay cool until lunchtime! I already had a banana and an apple, so I was sorted for lunch today. My evening meal was easier to source as Belfort would still be open when I got back.

I was giving a friend a lift again today and picked Emma up from Belfort. The weather forecast did not show any let up in the extreme heat covering the whole of Europe this summer. Temperature was due to hit the high 30's or even low 40's today which was going to be a big problem for me! I do not manage the heat well. I have my factor 50 umbrella with me so if I can get to the top, at least I can sit in the shade waiting for the race to arrive.

I had a target point to leave my car by the roundabout where the road heading towards the race route closed to all traffic except cycles, and I tried to park on the roadside. It was where I parked in 2017. A nice man came over from the houses opposite and said I could park in his drive instead! How kind is that! My car would be in the full sun all day unfortunately, but I was parked off the road in probably the best place in the whole area! 7.3 kilometres away from the start of the climb.

Emma did not have a bike. Fortunately, and for the first time as far as I am aware, there were fleets of buses running from the roundabout where I had parked, to the base of the climb for anyone without a bike! The charge for this was not too bad and better than walking but did have to be booked and paid for online, in advance. (note – I did not see this done anywhere else this tour which is a shame)

I set up my bike and cycled off. The ride to the base of the climb was very slightly uphill but still quite easy to ride. It only took me about 20 minutes. And then it is a right turn onto the climb, and it is straight up at a ludicrous gradient! The whole climb is only 7 kilometres, but the average gradient is 8.7%. There are two sections of flat and one downhill between kilometres 3 and 5, which really mess with the overall gradient. The top is 24%!! On Gravel!!

I was reduced to walking very quickly. That was not a surprise as I am so unfit post Covid, much heavier than I wanted to be post lock down and it was too hot! However, I know I can walk 7 kilometres even if it does take me two hours!

Post Covid, the race is still not back to the total party that it was before. There are not as many people making the effort to come to this climb today, although I still expect them all to be out again on Alp d'Huez in six days' time. There were also no people dressing up. I did not notice anyone doing that on the whole mountain which is such a shame. Hopefully, this comes back again soon too.

I stopped to talk to someone who had parked their van on the mountain three days earlier. They were well off the road, so the police had allowed them to stay. She was the person who advised me that 3 or 4 campervans had been moved off earlier that morning. She also knew she would not be able to get off the mountain later that day either as they would not be opening the road until the following morning!

There were hundreds of cyclists heading upwards. I would guess that 5% of them were on electric bikes! That was new. And great to see. They allowed people who would not normally have access to the mountain to get to where they wanted to be. Excellent. I even saw a very elderly gentleman (must have been 90 years old!) on an electric tricycle! I, however, was pushing my bike uphill! One day I hope to be able to ride here but not this year!

I finally managed to get to the point where the podium, the stands and the hospitality houses were set up. This was at the top of a 20% section where the route levelled off before the gravel started and the final 24% to the top. It was also where the public access finished! This is not unusual for a summit finish. All the ones I have done over the years have the final 500 to 1000 metres closed to the public.

I took a picture looking up the rest of the race route just to prove I had made it. There was still 700 metres to go to the top. Everyone cycling and walking up from here was directed off to the left of the route onto the grass behind the barriers. From there it was possible to get to the very top but that was such a steep climb. On grass! If the race climb was 24% then the pedestrian route was well over 30%. And that bit nearly beat me. I had locked my bike to a set of railings round the outside of a stand of saplings and tried to clamber up to the top. I made it eventually and took pictures from before and after the finish gantry. There were hundreds of people here already. There was a small gap between the barriers and the mountain which allowed people to watch along the final 350 metres but that was full.

I decided to head back down the too steep slope! Going down was so hard. I slipped and struggled back to my bike and was lucky not to end up rolling all the way to the bottom! How anyone did this in Cleats I have no idea.

The final 500 metres of the race route was full, and it was impossible to get to the barriers or walk back along the race route. My plan was to set up camp at about 600 metres to go. I was on the outside of a very gentle curve right against the barriers with a steep grass bank behind me preventing too many people joining me there and spoiling my view! I had an unobstructed view downhill for about 300 metres and uphill for another 200 metres to where the route turned the final corner. And I was on the gravel section which I had never seen before. In 2017 the race did not come up to this point. In 2019 I did not have my bike! Helicopter day.

I set up my usual camp and tied my Yorkshire flag to the outside of the barriers. Not sure how I got away with that, but the Gendarmes did not say anything, so it stayed. I sat down leaning against the grassy bank, eating a quite late lunch, and watching all sorts of people with exclusive access cycling up the gravel section. 3 or 4 ex pros, VIPs, and others who I had no idea who they were! The team cars were not allowed to come up this far. That meant that the team carers had to carry the kit required by the riders to the top on foot! Food, liquids, spare kit, wheels, loads of stuff. And very heavy!

There was a group of about eight people wandering about on the grassy areas all around the ski slope to the top, who were playing drums of assorted sizes. They were surprisingly good! And very enthusiastic! And loud! And they went on for ages before moving on to the next point and doing it over again! They certainly helped with the party atmosphere, but it was still difficult to interact with too many people as Covid has left a residual worry of catching it in crowds. My favourite pastime is talking to as many people as stand still long enough in English, or my dreadful French. Covid stopped so much of that this year.

The scenery was breath-taking! The view from the top out over the surrounding hills was beautiful. We were buzzed by a military plane four times too! Very loud. I sat under my umbrella watching a flock of large birds of prey just lazily wafting around on the breeze. And other people without a brolly melting in the extreme heat! There were people sat under the trees off to one side trying to keep cool. If you take nothing else, take some shade with you.

The caravan did not come up as far as I was today. It turned off just past the podium so it could not damage the gravel section. And probably because it was too steep!

When the race came past, I took some good videos of not only the poor guy dangling off the front and giving it everything he had as he came past me, but of the GC guys pegging him back by going so much faster! They caught him just before the finish line! Pogacar won again after a fabulous fight with Vingegaard. Their faces! The struggle, the effort, the speed was so visible to me at the roadside. On TV, the terrain looks flatter than it is, and the speed looks slower. I assure you, it is practically vertical, and they were going extremely fast!!

The rest of the race behind the GC guys was in pieces! The last rider home was only 22 minutes behind the winner which was very well done for the sprinters. I took as many photos of them as I could coming up much slower than the leaders and to get riders in these pictures even though I still just point and press. The view was amazing.

The riders by that time were also coming back down the mountain on the race route! All the teams' buses were at the foot of this climb as usual. It was funny to watch them coming down the gravel bit as others were still struggling up! Luke Rowe was sending showers of stones in all directions as he kept breaking and skidding (on purpose) on the way down. Knowing where to look is complicated and confusing but such fun! TV never shows this which is such a shame.

Once the final riders had reached the top, recovered a bit, and then set off downhill again, I packed up, retrieved my bike, and prepared to set off down the mountain. Not easy. There were thousands of us all trying to scramble down the grass towards where we could re-join the road part. There were people who had walked all the way up here which was impressive! The majority however had bikes. I wear Trainers as I am not a cyclist, but cleats made walking on the grass hard. People in Cleats were slipping and sliding all over the place.

The exit from the top of the mountain has two roads that join about 1 kilometre from the finish line. One is the race route and was where most of the crowd joined the way down. The other came from behind the podium and the hospitality houses, and was the exit for the team cars, and all the official vehicles which drive in front and behind the race. There are also at least thirty buses parked at the junction of the two roads for transporting race officials, marshals, police, VIP's, all the hundreds of people required to put on a bike race, and everything had to get off the mountain.

The police blocked one road so the VIPs could get off first, holding all the cyclists back for some unknown reason. They did not do this last time I was here. Wout Van Aert and Thibaut Pinot also got stuck with us after their visits to the podium and had to squeeze through to get to the front of the pack to get let out! Only at the tour!

I eventually escaped and cycled down. Even with being held up it was still quicker than driving. There is one thing the organisers get very right off this mountain. There is a forestry track that runs off the mountain, parallel to the race route road, with a junction only 500 metres from the place where all the cyclists are joining the route down. The tour sends most of the motorised vehicles down this track. The caravan, the buses, the team cars, everything. It means that the road we all cycle down is free of most vehicles. That makes an enormous difference to a nervous descender like me!

It is a quick descent even for me as it is not that long. And the rest of the ride to the car is also slightly downhill so easy to do. Emma beat me to my car though as she had watched the race come past from the foot of the climb and walked back from there. The fleet of buses for pedestrians was not going to start up again until much later allowing those who walked to the top time to get back down first, I assume. It is just a short drive from there to drop Emma of in Belfort, buy supplies in the nearby Supermarket, and get back to my B&B. I could have gone out to eat but a day pushing a bike up a mountain in extreme heat is way too tiring! As it was hot again today, dehydration is a big issue for me. I cannot carry more than four bottles of water and that is not enough. There was nowhere to get more today either. No campervans, no houses, no standpipes, nothing. I had left two bottles of water in the fridge, so it was just a case of drink constantly to try and rehydrate!

There are three mountains that are iconic in the Tour de France – The Col du Tourmalet, Alp d'Huez and Mont Ventoux. I have attempted to reach the summit of all of them more than once with zero success! I have tried the Tourmalet twice now. I managed to get within 2 kilometres of the top the second time, but I just could not go any further in 2021. Alp d'Huez was a huge step too far for my first attempt as I had managed to get to the top of two other HC mountains in the two days before trying the Alp! No chance! Second attempt was in 2022, the day after I reached the top of the Col du Granon, and way too hot!

Mont Ventoux is just too big! And way too hard to get to. And in 2016 it was too windy! But that is the one I will tell you about.

Thursday, 14th July 2016. Mont Ventoux.

It's Bastille Day. It is the big day! It's finally arrived and here I was planning to cycle up the biggest mountain the Tour goes to even if its top had been cut off! Mont Ventoux. Every tour fan knows Mont Ventoux. The wind that day was extreme, so the final 6 kilometres had been axed from the route leaving the finish at Chalet Reynard. That is still one hell of a challenge for a novice like me! Over 10 kilometres at an average of just under 9%!

I had managed to find a place to stay in Malaucene but that was as close as I could get. There is a road that runs from Malaucene to the top of Mont Ventoux, but this road will have been closed for two or three days prior to the race as this is used to get everything needed for the race up to the top of the mountain and back down afterwards. There is usually an entire media village planted on top of this mountain but because of the extreme winds today that had been moved off the mountain and parked in a car park outside Bedoin. The hospitality houses had been relocated to just below Chalet Reynard on to the road leading away from the mountain towards Soult. That road was also closed.

The barriers from the top of the mountain were still at the top! Way too many to move at such short notice. There is a campervan parking area that will have been full for at least a week and that was now above Chalet Reynard! And probably not very safe to be honest!

My plan for today was to drive as close as I could to the foot of the climb and just cycle the rest. I made it about 6 kilometres before the road shut! I still had over 10 kilometres left to go before I reached the base of Mont Ventoux. There was a Caveau or Wine shop on that junction that allowed people to park in their car park for the day for a small fee with the promise of a free bottle of wine when we got back! Anyway, I took my bike out of the car, set it up and rode off. The next 10 kilometres were so hard! I had to go over the Col de la Madeleine first and then it was just up and down all the way to Bedoin. On the way up the Col de la Madeleine, I had my first mechanical! My front Derailleur was not working properly, and it flicked my chain off! A whole peloton of riders stopped and sorted it out for me before riding off! Everyone looks out for everyone else at the tour. Thanks guys!

The WIND! It was awful! So Strong. Bedoin when I finally reached it was absolutely rammed with cyclists and walkers! And it was only 11 in the morning! The race was not due until around 5 ish.

The road then headed out of Bedoin a short distance to the actual foot of the climb proper. For the first few kilometres of the climb, the slope is around the 7% mark, which is possible for me cycling wise. I sat on the wheels of this big bloke on a mountain bike with great big fat tyres for about 3 kilometres. He kept the wind off me as it was a head / cross wind, and I could hardly move without him! Unfortunately, he was too strong a rider and eventually he left me behind! The wind was so strong I saw two or three riders blown clean off the road into the Cherry Orchard at the side! I also went into the cherry orchard but on purpose, to pick a handful cherries as they were just ripe and too tempting to pass up!

Once I got into the trees though I was able to continue riding onwards and upwards as the trees provided at least a bit of shelter, but it started to get steeper and steeper. With over 5 kilometres still to go it was way beyond me, so I had to get off and walk the rest. There was a lovely young man from Columbia in the same predicament as me in that cycling there was well out of our ability! So, we walked up together! He spoke excellent English and worked in Lyon! He was more interested in photography than reaching the top, so he stopped with about 2 kilometres still left to go to the lowered finish. There were hundreds of people still going up the mountain even though the race was not due for another 4 hours!

Some of the sights to be witnessed on the sides of the road are just so interesting and often very funny. There was a group of people all dressed up in medieval costumes who had built an entire castle out of cardboard! Five guys were dressed up as Tetrus cubes. There was another group who had dressed as Vicars, Nuns, and a Pope! I saw Didi the Devil who is quite famous among Tour fans! There was a Viking with a huge horned helmet on his head. I took as many pictures as I could of all the effort people had made just to sit at the side of the road for hours to watch 180 riders go past! You do sometimes notice these people on the TV coverage but there are thousands of them! You need to be there to see just what it is like.

I kept on walking and eventually made it to the 500 metres to go point which was as high as I could get without a pass! But I was still there, and it felt amazing. Mont Ventoux! I had done what I had set out to do all those months ago! I still felt good, and I think if the route had not been shortened, I might have made it to the top! Now I will have to wait until the route comes here again so I can find out!

There were thousands of people there and no barriers except for the final 500 metres. The race organisers usually have barriers set up for at least the final 2 kilometres if not more. I took some photos just to prove I had got there with my bike, then headed back down to around the 2 kilometres to go point where I had seen a good place to watch the race come by. It was a low 6 ft rocky cliff at the side of the race route, with a huge grassy bank on top of it. I parked my bike against the rocks and scrambled up on to the grass to set up camp. There was a young couple from Manchester there who had walked up from Bedoin. Again, lovely company waiting for the race to arrive.

The caravan did not come up to Mont Ventoux. Neither did the team buses. And the media village was in the valley! Way too windy. I found out later that the buses came up towards Chalet Reynard from the direction of Soult and they left that way too. There were still campervans clinging to the side of the mountain all the way to the top, but they will have been there for days! Most had been tied down but at least one had been blown over the side. Saw that on the news later that day! There are pictures on YouTube of TV people, including Chris Boardman, trying to stand up at the top of Ventoux that day. The wind was around 100 kilometres per hour at the top apparently. It was strong enough 6 kilometres down the mountain where I was!

This was the first stage that the couple from Manchester had seen so I tried to describe the caravan to them as they would not get the chance to see it! It is just not possible to convey the absurdity that is the caravan in words! You need see it for yourself.

We watched everyone still trudging and cycling up this mountain, the outfits, the parties, the sheer fun everyone has. Our little ledge became very full of people before the race arrived. So many people from all over the world to sit and watch a bike race with. We had quite a party on that grassy ledge!

When the race eventually came through, I had an unobstructed view looking down on the riders as they came past. I saw Thomas De Ghent leading the way up first from the breakaway. He is a great rider to watch as he attacks to get into the breakaway whenever he thinks there is a chance of the breakaway staying away to the finish. Today he was rewarded with an excellent win! I took some surprisingly good pictures from my vantage point. I even took one of Froome, Porte and Mollema absolutely steaming up the mountain having left the rest of the GC contenders behind! More on that later (although you already know what happened as it is probably the most watched clip of the race on YouTube, ever!)

So, the rest of the race came past, the Sprinters finally made it to the top and eventually the Broom wagon came through which is the last vehicle on the race each day. It was then time to ride back down. I totally flew down that mountain! My confidence has improved no end over the last few descents I have undertaken! Still slower than everyone else but it felt like I was going so fast! And I did not feel so scared or out of control. It only took me about 40 minutes to get all the way down, through Bedoin and on the road to Malaucene where I was staying. However, Mont Ventoux had not finished with me quite yet! The wind had become even stronger if that was possible. It was directly from the side, and I was leaning over into it just to stay upright! I have never felt so glad to be shortish and still quite heavy! The tall skinny brigade had to struggle to not end up blown into the ditch!

Through Bedoin the road turned full into the wind! I had to ride the 10 kilometres back to the car, into the ferocious head wind and up and over the Col de la Madeleine again! No Chance. I ended up walking the ups and cycling the downs! I had to pedal downhill as well, or I just stopped! I eventually got back to the car and went into the Caveau for the free bottle of wine. They had loads there and I had a good look round! I then set off back towards the hotel but stopped in Malaucene to buy something for dinner from the local shops as I was exhausted! I needed more than 2 weeks training to do what I had today and feel anyway fit enough to do anything other than collapse! My plan had been to eat in the hotel restaurant but decided that a long shower followed by a beer from the room's fridge (I had put a bottle in there the night before!) and a light dinner in the robe provided by the hotel was what I really needed. I had been snacking all day as it was, so I was not hungry. I was again covered in dust from all that wind and that was welded to my skin! It took ages to get it all off. I then turned on the TV and watched the astonishing scenes of Froome RUNNING up Mont Ventoux! Ridiculous! Funniest moment in Tour history I expect.

What a day though. My target had been to attempt to ride up Mont Ventoux from the moment I decided to buy my bike back in February. Mont Ventoux starts off OK, but then starts to quickly get steeper. It then gets even more steep and never lets up all the way up! It is AWESOME! I had taken pictures of the true summit and I think I may have managed to get all the way up but now to find out I will have to come back and do it again! I am looking forward to that.

Hints and tips.

Mountains stages are awesome! Mid stage mountains will allow you to get to the top, summit finishes will not. Mid stage mountains are, on average, less crowded with fewer people dressing up. Summit finishes are more crowded with more parties and more people dressing up. Both are worth doing.

The three iconic mountains will be crowded wherever they come in the stage!

Be prepared to wait for a long time for the race to come past. Take everything you need with you as you are unlikely to be able to get much if anything on the mountain.

Take a Brolly for shade. It will make the waiting so much more comfortable and less reliant on trees.

Take as much water as you can carry. It is possible to get more on Alpine mountains as they have excellent standpipes and there are also streams coming out of culverts there that you can use to pour over your head to cool down. I would not recommend drinking from these though!

Talk to people near you. They are all there for the same reason and it is such fun to talk to others from all over the world in whatever language you can manage.

Parking in the Alps is not easy. Roads are few and far between. Often, there is only one road away from which ever town you happen to be in so be prepared for delays if driving. The Pyrenees are a bit easier to manage.

Trains are impractical for both the Alps and the Pyrenees. Getting close to the foot of a mountains climb is unlikely.

Buses are possible although taking a bike on them I do not know about.

Take a bike. Electric or not, it will make your enjoyment that much more!

Starts

I love the starts! There is so much to see, so much to do and it is the best place to get close to everything and everyone. Seeing everything at the start in one go is not feasible though. There are 8 or 9 'zones' to a race start, each worth a visit, and usually laid out in a similar order for each start town.

The focal point of the start area is the sign on podium and everything else flows outwards from that. Every rider must sign on and since Covid, they all turn up as a team rather than on their own, in an order assigned by ASO. Each team is introduced to the waiting crowds. Marc Chauvet is the Podium Presenter who will interview at least one rider from each team in whatever language they are most comfortable! The podium also has a pre sign on show which is fun.

Other areas or zones are –

The Village Depart. This is accessible by ticket or invitation only and has various stalls or booths set up with local foods, local trades, plus tour sponsors stands and its own mini podium. It is all free once you are inside.

The Fan Zone. This is free to all and has loads of activities such as static bike races, spin the wheel games, children's bike riding obstacle courses, foods, sponsors trade stands, ASO trade stands, free Senseo coffee, so much to see and do!

The Paddock d'Equipes. This is the barriered off area for all the teams' buses and vehicles to park in to bring the riders and their bikes to the start. It is also only accessible by a pass, but you can still see and talk to so many riders and staff by just standing against the barriers round the outside.

The route between the Paddock and the Podium. The riders all must sign on. To get there they will cycle from the buses along a barriered section that is a good place to stand to see every rider up close although they do not tend to stop here. They will go past three times too which is fun.

The Depart Fictif. This is the start of the race where the riders all line up ready for the roll out.

The route between the podium (or sometimes the buses depending on the layout of the town) and the Depart Fictif. Again, a good place to see all the riders.

Artisan Markets. Not always there but sometimes the start town will set up a local produce specific market with local artisan producers displaying their wares. I love these!!

The Roll out route. This takes the riders to a safer place to start racing and can be many kilometres from the Depart Fictif.

The Depart Real. Often known as Kilometre zero where the true racing begins.

My first example is one of the most fun ones I did!

Saturday, 6th July 2019. Brussels. Grand depart.

I am in Brussels, in Belgium. I have never been to Belgium before and never been to the start of the very first stage of the tour before either. I have done starts on other tours and I love them! This one should be good as it is going to be used for two consecutive days this time instead of the usual one. That means everything seems a bit more permanent.

There is a great deal to see and do at all starts and I am lucky enough to have an access all areas pass for day one, courtesy of Team Sky. As I had arrived in Brussels the day before, I had already checked out what was going to be where at the start, and it was going to be huge!

The access to the Village Depart was through the Paddock d'Equipes. This is not always the case but made it easy for me to do both today. To get into it though was a bit of a faff! First, I had to go through a security check point into the Paddock d'Equipes. That is where I got a yellow tag put on my handbag to show it had no sharp objects or bombs! I am quite happy to go through any sort of checkpoint if it allows everyone to be safe and the race to continue! It is just a shame that it is necessary.

I then walked through the paddock to the Village entrance only to be advised that I needed a badge which was being given out at the initial check point! I was not the only one who did not have one. Many of us then traipsed back to the checkpoint where the queue had grown, only to be told we had to queue up and go through the checkpoint again. I was having none of that! I found the lady who should have been giving out the badges and I expect she gave me one just to get rid of me!

What to do first? The Paddock d'Equipes was empty at that point, 9.30 am, so I headed into the Village Depart. It was HUGE! Way bigger than any I had seen before. The Paddock d'Equipes was covering most of a massive carpark in front of the Royal Palace with the Village spread out along one side of it in the Parc de Bruxelles. This had lots of sort of roads crossing it everywhere and the village had fenced off three long roads at one end of the park. They had then put up all the booths and stalls along one side of each of these three roads. Each booth belongs to a different tour sponsor or local trader, and they want you to come in and talk to them. The booths are all different shapes and sizes, offering different things including trying out the wares they are trying to sell. Bikes, Zwift, Helmets, Gels, Power bars, loads of cycling paraphernalia, I think you can even get a loan!

These booths and stalls are excellent, and most are giving away different types of food and drink. One had fresh pastries with either sparkling wine, beer, juices, or soft drinks. Another was full of Belgian Chocolates. You could get sandwiches which were dainty with interesting fillings. There was a guy in a full chef's outfit, including the hat, making the most amazing miniature cups out of tempered chocolate, and then piping a coffee foam mixture into them to make them look like little cups of coffee. They were delicious! At each Village Depart there is always a central stall giving away chicken and chips, fresh fruit, diverse types of pastries and cheeses along with something local. This time it was freshly made Waffles on sticks! I spent quite a while wandering round there tasting as much of the food on offer as I could. I also had several cups of Senseo coffee from their stall in the middle of the three roads, which is excellent. And it is all free!

By a very dirty, lifeless pond in the centre of the Village Depart, ASO had set up a podium to interview whoever they could find. Tommy Voeckler was one of them. On a previous tour I had met Jonathan Edwards (triple jump Olympic Gold Medallist) who had insisted that I take a selfie with him rather than just his photo, and 'encouraged' me to take as many selfies as I could during this year's tour which I decided I would try and do. Tommy was my first one on this tour! I really enjoyed this challenge and took loads more throughout the 3 weeks! Most are rubbish because I am in them, but they were fun to get! Tommy is just lovely. I was wearing my Yorkshire Lasses cycling top and we spoke about Yorkshire and the Tour de Yorkshire, which he had just won, for ages.

The King of Belgium was in the Village Depart as was the Prince of Monaco. They were easy to spot as they had full entourages! I freely admit, I had to ask someone who they were. I should really have known; especially has I had seen the Prince before at one of the starts in 2015! I also spotted Eddie Merckx but there was no getting near him either this tour. The place was crowded, and all the stalls were doing a roaring trade. I could have had Alcohol in the form of local wines if I wanted but it was only 10 am! Others though, partook.

Eventually I left the village as there was just too much chocolate! I walked back into the Paddock, and I spotted Bradley Wiggins walking across the carpark before the buses arrived. I asked him if I could take a photo with him and he said yes, but I had to practically run alongside him to do it. He did not even slow down at all! Still, expert use of my Brolly enabled me to get a surprisingly good picture! You can see the edge of it in the picture. Jens Voight! I met the Jensie! Talking to him is so easy! Making him stop talking is another matter!! I love him! Tommy, Brad, and Jens! My tour is now complete, and the race has not even started yet!

What to do now? The teams had not arrived yet so I wandered round the barriers at the edge talking to as many people outside the Paddock as I could. Again, there were people from all round the world. I love finding out where they come from, why they are there, what their plans are, anything really. An hour of chatting makes the time fly! My French is pretty rubbish, my Spanish and Italian non-existent but I still manage to converse with so many people. Belgians Love their cycling. Talking to them is great as they have all been watching cycling forever and know so much about everything to do with it.

The Paddock this stage was huge and was going to fit all the buses, cars, and vans in easily. This is not always the case! Each team has one large bus, two cars for the 2 DS's, one car to drive ahead of the race to report on conditions before the riders reach each section, plus at least two and sometimes four other vehicles doing heaven knows what! Watching the convoy of buses and vehicles in team colours arrive is spectacular. I love seeing the cars that have the bikes on top! They look just like prickly hedgehogs driving down the road.

Once they had all parked up it was then a case of seeing who was about that I could accost! I have made loads of friends on various teams over the years as everyone is approachable and very friendly, except Movistar who I have never managed to get near! Their bus is always surrounded by Colombian fans. I chatted with George, Xabi and Roderick from Team Sky, Russ Ellis, a Photographer who lives near me, Daniel Frebe from ITV who I accost all over France each year, and Ashley House from Eurosport. Also had a quick chat with Neil Stephens of UAE team and John Trevorrow who is with the Mitchelton Scott team. It is so nice meeting up with the same people each tour, especially if they remember your name! Makes my tour!

I had decided to take pictures of bikes today. I had access to every bus (except Movistar!), and I like to post them for the Yorkshire Lasses Facebook page! They are so cool to look at, but they all look small to me! No idea why I have that perception, but they just appear small. I also spoke to a couple of the mechanics and staff as they were all just so approachable! I am not a technical bike nerd although I have managed to change a tyre once, but I am interested in how everyone's day unfolds. What time they start, what they see of the race, do they hand out bottles at feed stations, do they travel in the cars with the DS's, do they get car sick!?? Sometimes it could be just a chat about the weather.

Eventually the riders started emerging from their buses and I set off to take photos of them, which is fun, without impeding them in any way. I did take a picture of one of the Yates twins as he stepped off his bus. No idea which one! One was supposed to wear Red shoes and the other Blue, but this one was in White shoes so how was I supposed to figure out who it was! I took a photo, hopefully I can work it out who it is later, but I doubt it! (it is no good, I have no idea which one it is!). I took a great picture of Richie Porte. And one of Bauke Mollema. I have spoken to Dan Martin often over the years, and I took a lovely picture of him. Also managed to get one of Michael Matthews. I have still not got the picture I want of Valverde, but I will get one eventually.

The media also arrived at the same time as the buses unfortunately. There are hundreds of them! Most are quite nice, but others are just not. They constantly barge the fans out of their way so they can get a picture of a bike cable or an interview with a random person. And any cyclist trying to get anywhere once they leave the safety of their bus is often hampered, both physically and often mentally. The fans without access to the paddock who have been patiently waiting against the barriers for a glimpse of their favourite riders, are treated with total contempt. It is such a shame. However, most teams try and compensate for this by interacting with as many fans as they can get to. That is what makes the whole experience so great. You will get to talk to at least one rider, and many of the team staff, at any start, from inside the Paddock or from outside the barriers. I love cycling!

The riders must ride to the sign on Podium first, then come back to the buses, and finally leave to ride to the start line which on this start was about 2 kilometres away. I placed myself near the exit to the paddock and the route to the Podium. I saw everyone ride pass! I took loads of pictures, and spoke to anyone I recognised, most answered! And they all went past three times! Amazing.

After they had all left the paddock for the final time, I went back into the Village and sat on a comfortable sofa, drinking Senseo coffee, eating various food items, (yes it was mostly

Belgian chocolate!) watching the race set off on a giant TV screen. I love the starts! It is all about people there, both from inside the teams, from the nice media and from the fans from all over the world.

—◦◦◦—

Monday, 6th July 2021. Start in Albertville

I had stayed in a lovely apartment last night about 10 kilometres from today's start in Albertville. I had been there for three nights as the rest day was yesterday. The place was exactly like a picture from a jigsaw puzzle of an alpine village! And I had spent the entire day doing absolutely nothing! Proper rest day this time.

My young friend Emma was with me again today. The only way to describe how I know her is to mention that I rescued her in Brussels in 2019! Long story which I may tell one day!

My plan was to see the start in Albertville by parking in any of the three places I had identified as possible. In fact, none were reachable! It is all guess work before you turn up but if you have studied the race route and the layout of the town beforehand, then it is much easier to sort things out if they go wrong! In the end I just followed my instincts, drove until I could not go any further and parked on a wide path! The police watched me do this and took no notice so I assumed it would be ok. It was fortunately! And the position was perfect. We were within 500 metres of the entrance to the Paddock d'Equipes and as far from the podium as it was possible to be and still be in the same start town! Today's start layout was in one long line, so each zone followed on from the next. That is a long way realistically to walk but it does make things easy to find!

We were also a bit early so had plenty of time to wander all the way past the paddock and towards the Depart Fictif. Between the 4 lane road the paddock was on, and the river running parallel, was a pretty park area. Just past this there was an artisan market set up by the local farmers which was fabulous. One stall was just for apple products with cider, puree, juice etc, all of which they just wanted people to try so we did! It was delicious.

There was so much to see and try – hundreds of local cheeses, local breads, spirits, pasta, handmade greetings cards, jams and preserves, Macaroons, and some amazing dried and cured meats. I could not buy the cheese as I had no fridge, but the dried meats would travel fine in their packaging, so I did buy three types of these! And the Macaroons were delicious!

Next, we came across a huge fan park which was full of people which is so good to see. This was opposite the sign on podium which was inside the barriers. The fan park had all the usual stuff there, including the free Senseo coffee stall which it would be rude to ignore! They had built a small circuit for the children to race on! Young children on balance bikes. Lovely to see kids having fun on bikes.

There was a show on at the Podium as we passed. They had acrobats, dancers, and a magician! The trick cyclist is back too! He is great but he could not use people from the crowd today in his act due to covid restrictions, so he used inanimate objects to jump over instead!

A bit further on from here was the Depart Fictif. That was already quite full of people waiting there to see the rider's line up and then ride off. That is all that happens there so I rarely watch this bit unless I can access it easily without having to sit beside the barriers for hours! The riders line up and then they are gone! 5 minutes tops! And usually much less!

What I did not find was the Village Depart. No idea where that was but it cannot have been too far off to one side of everything else!

When the buses arrived, after the caravan had passed through, we were able to walk up and down the park side of the paddock and had an excellent view of everything we wanted to see. All the buses were parked on the same side, away from the park. I spoke to the usual suspects again, Gary from ISN, George and Rod from INEOS and a new contact from DQS team, Phil Lowe. He is their Press officer, and he has been warned that I will accost him all over France in the following days! He did not seem to mind but we will see! Rod gave us a couple INEOS face masks which really help with getting to places we are not really supposed to get, so great!

The Paddock access was heavily restricted due to Covid Rules which meant that the only people in the paddock were the teams themselves. No Journos or VIP guests at all. This meant that you could see everything! This made everything better for the fans even if I could not get into the Paddock myself. Everyone was wearing Masks which did make identification a bit tricky! The tour had arranged that all the media had little barriered boxes to stand in. The riders then stopped outside the boxes for their interviews if they decided to do interviews rather than the media coming to the riders and teams! The media all had microphones on long poles so they could keep their distance from the riders.

Only downside here is that the interview boxes are situated near the podium and its loudspeakers! Hearing anything over these is difficult at the best of times so trying to do interviews from six feet apart with that noise going on must have been extremely difficult!

I set up shop outside the ISN team bus as it was near the junction of the paddock and the run to the podium, and I would be able to see most riders heading to and from the sign on podium up near the start. I took so many pictures! All of them came out ok today and I think I must now have a photo of every rider on the race! I got a wave from Alaphilippe, a great close up of Cav, and excellent one of Froomey. Also, one of Froomey, Glen and Rod having a catch up! Froomey also came over and signed a copy of his book that someone had brought with them! He is so great with the fans. Finally had a wave from Tao! That is an excellent picture! And another laugh with Luke Rowe! Wout Van Aert stopped right next to me to speak to someone as well! What a great start that was.

The riders all had to come past three times as well. Everything in the Paddock d'Equipes was so relaxed without the media and VIPs. Just the teams so the riders had time to stop and talk to whoever they wanted to. The crowds were also smaller as Covid has kept so many people away this year.

Once the riders had set off, we stayed to watch some of the infrastructure begin to be dismantled ready to head off to the next day's start town. That is also interesting. Even the Stencilled sponsors names on the road are burned off! The Buses all drove away along the race route behind the riders which meant I could drive straight to the main road to Geneva which ran alongside the race route for about 30 kilometres. We never saw the riders again though on my drive!

Tuesday, 4th July 2017. Start in Mondorf les Bains

I stayed in Mondorf last night. What an amazing hotel! Rather than being an hotel with a bit of a Spa, it was a massive Spa with a bit of an hotel attached! And I had free access with my hotel booking. The spa complex was outdoors set in landscaped gardens. There were at least eight different saunas like large cabins scattered around the landscaped grounds, each with a different heat, or scent, or something! There was a huge steam room which was partially underground. There were three pools! One was an infinity pool lined with jacuzzi beds looking out over the second pool. This had an island off to one side with rapids!

The main building had two restaurants, a bistro café, massage centres, therapy places, gyms, conference rooms, sports halls, everything you could think of for a spa and sports complex!

The final pool started in this building with wall jets, bubble beds, waterfalls, etc, then you could swim through a tunnel and access the rest of this pool outside! With more water jets, and waterfalls etc! All the water was hot as it was a thermal spa! I loved it! Only downside was you were not supposed to wear anything in the Saunas! No costume! I could not do that, so I kept mine on and got a few scowls from official looking people! I pretended not to understand their French!

Tonight was my second night staying in this hotel as I could easily get to the end of the previous stage from here and back without crossing the race route. I had arrived back at the hotel about 6 pm that evening, after watching the end of the days stage in Longwy and decided to check out what was happening at the race route which ran round the outside of the spa! There were armies of people putting barriers up everywhere, the hospitality village was going up, all the start media were arriving, and there was also a Fan Zone going up in the centre of the town that was already in full swing with live music, drinks and food stands and all sorts of things going on. The start podium was right in the middle of everything. This year it is a huge stage with side wings housing giant TV screens with mobile TV cameras attached to capture everything that happened on the stage. It was bigger than last years, I think. When it arrived, it was all folded up to the size of an articulated lorry trailer. I stopped to watch it being 'unfolded' to become the podium!

The Paddock d'Equipes was huge! The car park they were taking over was so big!! And they were surrounding the whole area with barriers! This construction, organisation and planning undertaking is fascinating to me! Although the draw of the Spa was too much and by 9 pm I was in the infinity pool, on a jacuzzi bed, looking up at the cloudless sky full of stars!

I packed up and left the hotel around 9 am the following morning, leaving everything in my car ready to leave later in the day and headed off to the start areas. The whole town was buzzing! There were people everywhere, and loads going on. I spotted Andy Schleck with his daughter in the Fan Zone. Mondorf had also sent up three giant hot air balloons by then which, as there was no wind, were just hovering over the town!

There was so much going on at the Sign on Podium / stage including a team of young riders who the compare introduced to the crowds. There was also a trick cyclist who was good! The hospitality village (Village Depart) was in full swing too but that was too far away to see into, on the opposite side of the Paddock d'Equipes (still huge!). I must try and get one of the entry bracelets somehow but not actually sure how. I will work that out one day!

There was just so much stuff that ASO transported into the area via giant lorries and built round the town that it is something that everyone who watches the Tour on TV should see at least once! All the lorries then parked on the outskirts of the town, well out of the way of any tour TV coverage. These lorries come in straight after the race leaves, pack it all up again and move it all to the next stages start. It is just fascinating to a planner like me.

I spoke to loads of people while awaiting the arrival of the teams. One cyclist had just finished canoeing for a week in the Alps. Two others were part of the technical bike support crew for an ultra-triathlon taking place in France somewhere or other in the following week.

The area cordoned off for the teams was vast. I took pictures of it before it filled up with all the team's vehicles. When the teams arrive, they bring twenty-two team buses which are impressive, and then each team has a fleet of between 4 and 6 cars which comes to at least one hundred cars! Most teams have vans as well with the bikes or kit in. Each bus then puts out a barrier behind which the bikes are set up for the riders for that stage. The area needed for all this to park up is huge. The vast carpark allocated this time was big enough for all of them with room to spare. This is not always the case. I have been to some where they do not all fit and have to park wherever they can at the roadsides. And one where they could get the buses in but not back out as the exit was too small. Love the tour!

The bikes themselves are so sleek and elegant! And they look small which I find very surprising. Each team has a different make or model depending on who their sponsors are and there are many assorted colours even within each team if a rider has a special paint job done for a specific reason. Greg Van Avermaet had a Red BMC bike with Gold Accents on as he was the current Olympic champion which was a lovely looking bike! The bike of Sergio Henao as the Columbian National Road Race Champion was beautiful! Still not sure about the AG2R bikes though. Their colours are Light Blue, Beige, Brown and White. Their cars are also in the same team colours, and they look dreadful!

The riders are all safely ensconced on their team buses at this point where they have the pre-race team briefings. After that they all hop on their bikes and struggle through the fans and journo's clogging up the entire paddock to the sign on podium. It is a struggle too! There are riders everywhere going in both directions and the VIP pedestrians just do not look where they are going! Having said that, I must find a way to get one of the passes into this area! I did manage to get some good pictures though as even from outside the barriers, the riders come really close!

Not all the vehicles follow the race. Each team is allowed just two cars each to follow the riders, and these are bristling with spare bikes! And stuffed full of spare wheels! Each one takes a mechanic and one of the 2 Director Sportifs (DS's) who are the teams race tacticians. Most of the other vehicles go off ahead of the race. These drop off and later collect the Swannies (helpers) who stand at the side of the road waiting for the riders ready to hand out water bottles, and food as they ride past. In Team Sky (the other teams all do this too)

Rod Ellingworth is the guy who goes ahead to give feedback on anything that the road book cannot detail and the weather as it might impact the race tactics. He drove last year's signature vehicle of the Ford Mustang. This year he has a Ford Escort! It is still the latest model and I have to say it looks good! Anyway, I spoke to Rod last year in Andorra. Naturally when I spotted him this time, I said Hi again! He remembered me! And he said that they had been wondering if I would be there again this year! He was interested in how I was and what I was doing for this year's tour. He is just such a lovely man! I know my story is good PR for Team Sky, but it meant my life to me and to have someone that interested to remember my face was the nicest thing that has happened to me in a long time!

I was able from where I had positioned myself to get to the roll out route through a short alleyway! I nipped through here to watch the caravan go past. It is even bigger than last year and still totally insane! A group of about forty local schoolkids had come out to the side of the road and they had a wonderful time collecting as much rubbish as they could from the tat thrown out! It was great fun just to watch them! I intended to come back here to watch the roll out go past as well which was a bonus.

The start in Mondorf was a good one! I was able to stand by two of the buses and at a pinch point in the middle of the paddock. I could see and interact with the riders and staff at the Sky and BMC buses and see the riders from about half the other teams come through the pinch point! And then after the riders left for the start, they were going to roll out all round Mondorf for almost 8 kilometres before they came back to the other end of the little alleyway I had found! I could also see them on the roll out as well! Unusual but excellent!

I took lots of pictures from my vantage point with a good one of Romain Bardet. I still have not managed to get one of Contador yet. Or Valverde. Both are always surrounded by Journos so my view of them both has been blocked each time. I spoke to loads of people just standing by the barriers as we watched the riders going back and forth between the buses and the sign on podium. I could even see one of the TV screens on the Podium from where I was, so I could see what was happening there as well! It is a bit of a free for all on the podium to be honest!

I was in full point and press mode with my camera, so I was lucky to get as many pictures as I did with riders in them. Watching the riders from Sky and BMC warming up was new for me this year. I had not seen that done before. Fascinating.

I decided to watch the actual start on the big screen on the Sign on Podium which I do not usually get to do as the layout has to be right for it to work. That way I knew exactly when the race rolled off and how much time I had to get to where I wanted to watch the riders on the roll out.

I nipped through the alleyway to the road running alongside the Spa boundary to watch them roll past. I was at a wonderful place to catch the riders on the roll out on a straight piece of road just after a tight corner. The peloton might have come passed at a slow pace for them, but you could still sort of 'feel' the power of the riders and a sort of bow wave in front of them. You just do not get that from the TV! I tried to video this bit but messed that up completely! They were gone in seconds!

I then hung around a while to watch the Tour infrastructure start being dismantled as I could not get out of the carpark let alone the town until after 1.30 when the roads re-opened.

The team buses and remaining vehicles all had to get out of the Paddock d'Equipes! They were all packed away and rolling within 15 minutes of the race leaving! Then the lorries returned with the army of people to collect the barriers and put them on the lorry trailers. This was all done by hand! No machines to lift anything!

The Village Depart had also closed and was being dismantled. I watched the Podium being folded up, the lorry being driven up, hitched to the trailer, and driven off all in the space of about 40 minutes! The Fan Zone was still going strong though. That was mostly staying in Mondorf as it was their equipment supplemented with a few extra stalls from the tour organisers. I bought my lunch there before heading to my car and trying to get out of town!

Hints and Tips –

Watching the tour arrive and set up overnight is fun! It is a huge example of logistics at work.

There is often something organised by the host town the night before the race with all sorts of things going on. Food stalls, music concerts, dances, competitions, all worth a visit.

The teams all arrive around 2.5 hours before the start time. Seeing all the vehicles turn up and often squeeze into ridiculously small car parks is great.

The Caravan Publicitaire, consisting of hundreds of floats, will frequently go through the Paddock d'Equipes on its way to the start area and is seriously bizarre!

The preshow on the podium is always good. I watched someone painting a brilliant picture of Raymond Poulidor one year, and there is always a trick cyclist who is good. They had a magic show once. And a troupe of Can-Can girls in fabulous costumes. All sorts that happen between 3 and 2 hours before the start.

Getting there by train and by bus is typically easy. By car is often ok too but will require a bit more walking. Getting away is also easy if you are not going the same way as the race!

Starts are usually between 11.30 and 13.30. This will then give you the rest of the day to do whatever you want – Drive to another stage, have a good look at the start town, even sometimes go to the finish if you are incredibly lucky!

3

Sprint Finishes.

These, like the starts, have zones. They are simpler to describe but each has its own merits. And there is no way to see the race from more than one point at any one finish. To see them all will take more than one stage finish.

So far, I have watched potential sprint finishes from 1 kilometre to go, 500 metres to go, 250 metres to go, and 50 metres to go. I have also watched from after the finish line. Sprints from between 250 metres to go and the finish line are amazing to feel, hear, and experience the speed, but too fast to see anything. The 1 Kilometre point is slower but at least you can see them! 500 metres is awesome! So fast but you can still just about see them coming past. After the finish line is one of my favourite places to watch from as often you can get within 10 metres of the finish line, have a splendid view, then watch the interviews if they still do the media boxes set up post Covid and to the buses if you are lucky! Or to watch the podium presentations as these are normally just after the finish line.

If you do opt to see a sprint finish, be prepared to wait! The closer you get to the finish, the earlier you need to get there to be able to get any view of the race.

Saturday, 6th July 2018. Fontenay-le-Comte

I am going to be in the very small town of Fontenay-le-Comte today. I was staying about an hour away near a town called Les Herbiers as that was a central position for the first three stages of this year's tour. The race was due about 5 pm so I had loads of time today.

I arrived in Fontenay-le-Comte around 11 am and managed to park about 20 minutes' walk from the town centre on the main road into town which had parking areas all along either side. There was unfortunately no shade, but I was lucky in that the sun moved behind the houses later, so my car was not too bad in the fierce heat. I walked towards the race area. The whole area around the finish was cordoned off so to get within 2 kilometres of anything you had to go through security check points. I had never had to do this before and never seen the race route cordoned off like this, but it is an unfortunate sign of the times we live in, I guess. Still, it did not hold anyone up and it made no difference to me. (note – I have never had to do this at any other start I have been to since then)

Just to the right as I passed through the check point was a fan zone in full swing so I thought I would start my day there. It had taken over a sort of town square which was alongside a river and next to a sports complex. There was a large stage at one end of the square with a giant TV screen at the other. Along each of the sides there were numerous stalls set up by local clubs and societies selling all sorts of goodies. I had a wander round these which were mostly selling food related items, Ice cream, drinks, sandwiches, also T-shirts, hats, general club items and wares.

I decided to have my lunch at the stall run by the local Martial Arts group. They had a BBQ lit out the back of a vast tent cooking all sorts of meat products which smelt very inviting. For 10 Euro, I got half a melon, a large basket of chips, one sausage (a foot long one at that!), half a baguette (obviously) and a dish of fruit salad! I thought the small plastic beaker contained Apple Juice which would have been nice! I also bought a beer for two euro as it was extremely hot, and I was technically on holiday. They had erected two seating areas next to the cooking tent, one with a cover which was packed and one without which was empty. That was not a problem for me as I had my brolly for a sunshade!

40

I could see the big TV screen from where I was sitting, which was showing the Race, so I just sat there for over an hour. On the stage the live entertainment started up with a rock band which was OK if not brilliant. Once they had finished their set though, a local "group" dressed in local costumes playing local instruments started up! They were dreadful! They had French bagpipes which were all drone and no tune, an accordion like thing which was not in tune with everything else, a sort of recorder, tambourines and bongo's and they sang or chanted stuff that was never in a million years going to resemble music! And they decided to wander round the square later and inflict this din on everyone! It was awful!

Anyway, remember the apple juice? I took a swig of that, and it was strong Schnapps!! And I had a whole plastic beaker of it! It was delicious! And all for 12 Euros total! I freely admit that I drank it! It was going to be another 4 hours at least before I had to drive again so I should have been ok by then. It did mean I could not get another beer though!

I headed through the sports complex towards the Race Route around 3 pm and just caught the Caravan going past. I am sure there were even more floats than last year still throwing tons of tat to the waiting fans with the same inane tunes blaring out. It is such fun though and really makes the visit to watch the tour so different from every other sporting event. Watching three teenage boys physically fighting over a sachet of washing liquid about sums up the madness of the caravan for me. I totally love it!

I walked along the side of the route which was barriered off on both sides for at least 2 kilometres to the finish and it was packed with people waiting for the race to arrive. I set up camp at around the 500 metres to go point under my brolly getting hotter and hotter! Temperature was in the high 30's all day today. Others again wilted visibly without any shade.

I had not managed to talk to many people today either. The atmosphere was not nice at all. Unfortunately, due to the appalling French Press, they had got the casual bike race watcher so wound up with their mis reporting and frankly made up headlines that there was a great deal of booing directed towards Team Sky in general and Froome in particular. Froome crashed around 10 kilometres from the finish and when this was announced over the tannoy, many of the crowd cheered! That would never happen in Italy or Spain as they know their bike racing but too many of the casual French watchers unfortunately in general do not.

The race eventually came past. Fernando Gaviria won the bunch sprint in his first ever start at the tour on his first stage which is impressive at only 22 years old! However, I saw none of this as they still just go too fast and are a blur of colours! There is no way to work out individuals but still better than at the 50 metres to go point! The other senses are overloaded! The noise of the bikes, the shouting (and Swearing!), the air that is displaced as they come past can be felt buffeting you, but you just cannot process the sight of them fully. And taking pictures or videos? I missed them all again! But its ok as you can watch that on TV later!

Next were a few stragglers which included Froome, Porte and Yates although again they went too fast to be identified at the time. It did mean that Froome was not booed as he rode past as no one knew it was him! I did spot Quintana and Bernal behind them though as they were in a group of just four riders and not going so fast. Bernal was booed as he was in Sky kit!

After that the riders came in in dribs and drabs until the final rider came past in a terrible mess. He was covered in blood as he had obviously crashed hard. His name as I found out later was Lawson Craddock from America riding for the EF Education First team. He was unsure if he could continue due to his myriad injuries but decided that he would request for sponsorship for every stage he managed to complete! He would then donate this to the velodrome in New Orleans that had been destroyed by the Hurricane. He raised thousands of dollars as he made it all the way to Paris somehow!!

I tried to find my way back to my car after the race, but that was not as easy as it sounds! Most of the barriers had by then been removed and that changes the whole perception of where you are! I knew I was near the church though, so I found it eventually! Then a short drive back to the amazing Gite I was staying in.

That was it for my first day at this year's tour. I could have struggled towards the Podium but as Gaviria was going to be the only rider there, I decided to meander back to the car and head home. I was overheated and a bit dehydrated (I blame the Schnapps) and the heat was set to continue for days yet.

Friday 10th July 2015. Fougeres.

The Chambre d'Hotes was just a lovely place to stay. The room was comfortable, and the breakfast provided the next morning was simply perfect with eggs, fruit, cheese, all sorts of things to choose from and all so fresh! I had plenty of time to enjoy it as I had decided that I would skip the start, so I could see the end instead. I had had trouble on stage 5 trying to get from the Intermediate Sprint point to the finish and failed miserably! What with road closures, nowhere to park, and not enough time, I made the decision last night, so I was much more relaxed this morning.

It was due to be another sprint finish, so I decided that I wanted to see them go past before the finish to see just how fast they could go! I had watched from after the finish before which had been great, but I wanted to see from around the 200 meters to go point this time where the sprinters really let rip.

Livarot is 145 kilometres from Fougeres on the direct route, but this also happened to be the race route! I had to go on the main road all around the outside for an extra 40 kilometres to be able to get to Fougeres at all! This did not take any longer though as it was an autoroute all the way!

I arrived in Fougeres and just abandoned the car as close as I could get to the race route. It is relatively easy to do in such a big town as you just follow the road closed (Rue Barre) signs until the road closes, then find somewhere to park! At least that is what I did in Fougeres.

This time having made the decision as to what I wanted to see, I stocked up on drinks and food from the multitude of stalls around the finish area and went to the 200 metres to go point and just sat and waited. I had a puzzle book with me and did that for a few hours! It was a bit warm out there today, but the Vittel guys were driving up and down the road spraying everyone with cold water and handing out thousands of free bottles of water. Very handy. I will need an umbrella as a sunshade if I come again though as I am not used to the heat!

The crowds were at least three deep along the barriers with still 2 hours to go to the race arriving. There were more people arriving all the time, who then started trying to push in to get a better view. This is not fun! The final hours wait was stressful. At the 200 metres to go point there is a sign erected by the race organisers which has a heavy weighted stand to keep it upright. I used this to stand on a save my place. The sign itself provided a bit of shade as well which was very welcome. Sharp elbows, a bit of weight, determination and a lot of bloody mindedness are required to keep you place once you have found it.

I watched the caravan come past 90 minutes before the riders were due. It is complete madness. I am sure that some of the people standing at the barriers are only there to watch the Caravan! I am sure some left after it had passed. The people on the floats throw their sponsors gifts out over the heads of the crowds rather than at them which is fortunate. Being hit by a key ring is not nice!

After that, other sponsors started walking up and down the finish straight dressed in strange costumes giving out all sorts of things. Fruit, small salami type sausages, Haribo, t-shirts, caps, pens, keyrings, and even strange oversized blue glasses!

When the riders came past, I held up my camera and just pointed and hoped! I missed them totally as I found out when I got back to the hotel! The speed at which they came past was amazing. And the noise! It was just too fast to take anything in properly but such an experience! Cavendish won although I had no idea! There is no chance of seeing that as they are gone in milliseconds! You just cannot get the full experience from the TV pictures. The speed, the noise, the shouts, the pressure wave that goes in front of them! But it is just too fast to register what you are seeing. The Sprinters shoot past then everyone else including the GC riders come past at a slightly slower speed but still seriously fast! There are then loads of stragglers, the lead out men, the breakaway guys, the domestiques for the GC guys, and anyone who is injured. They are followed in by hundreds of cars and motorbikes! Way too many motorbikes in fact. They cannot all be essential to the race surely.

It took ages to get away from where I had been all day as the whole place was rammed! I did get to the area of the Presentation podium, and I saw Froome get his Yellow Jersey back as Tony Martin had abandoned. But I was too far away! Cavendish had won the stage and I watched him get his winners prizes as well. A huge cheer went up when Daniel Teklehaimanot was presented with his Polka Dot Jersey as Mountains point leader. He is the first rider in the peloton from Eritrea and the first Black African to hold a classification leaders Jersey. Lovely to see that and the photo I took came out well too even though I was using a zoom function, and he is still a small dot in the photo!

That was a long, stressful day to end up watching the riders sprint past for all of 2 seconds! I am not sure it is worth it. Watching from after the finish, I had a much better understanding of what had happened and a better view of the riders than I had at 200 metres to go. But the other senses triggered did make it interesting. Will I do that again? Unlikely. I have done it now and there are better ways to spend a day at the tour!

I stayed in a Chateau that night! It was fabulous! But it was also a bit out of the way and the nearest village had closed by the time I arrived! Even the MacDonald's closes before 7 pm! I could not get any food anywhere. I had to make do with Madeleines, Haribo and other edibles that the caravan had thrown out. I will need to take emergency rations if I come again as it seems this is not unusual for France. The room I had was just huge with what felt like an acre of floor space. It had a massive bed against one wall with two huge solid wood wardrobes on another, a lovely wooden dressing table, a small table and chairs, and a proper old-fashioned chaise longue. The bathroom was separate with a big bath which was just what I needed. There were also two full length windows looking out over the beautiful grounds. The entrance hall was spectacular with solid wood panelling all over the walls. The wooden staircase was something to behold. All carved and curved along one side of the hall. What a place even though I had had a dreadful time trying to find it!

Saturday, 13th July 2019. St Etienne.

The race route this year was a strange one. After a brief detour to the Jura mountains for stages 5 and 6, the next 6 days were all flat, with expected sprint finishes. It was like a very long transition phase to get to the Pyrenees! The organisers had also decided to make the first rest day after stage 10 rather than stage 9 as it normally is. I am not a fan of Sprint finishes so figuring out how to get the most out of these next days was complicated. The end of stage 8 and the start of stage 9 were both in St Etienne. If I stayed in St Etienne for the finish and the start, I could then head to Albi for the next stage final and the rest day.

To get to St Etienne should have taken about 4 hours from Belfort. Unfortunately, Lyon was in the way. I have no idea how many sets of roadworks there were on nearly every road going round Lyon, but I ended up having to go on a 60 kilometre detour just to find a road that was still moving.

The hotel in St Etienne when I finally arrived, was basic but clean. I also had a small kitchenette with a kettle. I could not get their kettle to work though so I just used my travelling one. The hotel was cheap but did have a parking space. They provided coffee and hot chocolate which was nice. The area of St Etienne I was in was a bit seedy and run down but it had a small park with a playground in the middle which was full of families even at 10 pm! I never felt uncomfortable or worried there at any time.

Breakfast was OK with a reasonable choice including some cereals today. Lots of bread as usual but they did have some nice tea as well. There were quite a few people in the very plastic orientated dining hall this morning included three men from England in full Lycra who were going to cycle out to one of the hills on the route to watch the race come past. They also were not fans of sprint finishes. I had investigated the same option but the roads to get there were not going to be closed and were big, fast roads. Not my idea of fun.

I left the hotel around 10 and got on a Tram (all free while the tour was in town) and got off near where the race ended today. I was staying in the south of the city and the start was in the north. The tram ride went right through the centre of the city and all the way to the end of the line out again. From the tram stop, there was only about 200 metres to the race area. The tram stop was specifically for fans wanting to go to a St Etienne football match which was where the tour had set up.

The first place I came to was the Fan Zone. This was quite a large area today with stalls, activities, and competitions spread out over a paved plaza. The stalls are random with one stall selling past and present team kits. Another booth was for Bio Products available via LeClerc. There was a stall just selling energy products.

Some of the competitions were set up on Swift bikes. People could test themselves against professionals' timings, or against the rider next to them. That was all free with prizes on offer. This was all next to the race route at the 50 metres to go point on the course.

All the barriers for the final 2 kilometres were in place already. The barriers were the new ones designed so that they did not have any feet projecting into the rider's path. The bonus here was that they sloped away from the course keeping the spectators back from the riders. I hope this works as well as it looks like it should.

I walked towards the finish line where the finishing touches were being made to the timing gantry. This had been brought in on its own tailer and unfolds into the gantry we see across the race route. The photo finish camera is set up separately and must be aligned to match the white line that will be drawn on the road.

Before anything is drawn on the road, the tarmac is painted black to hide any road markings and create a good contrast to the advertising which is then stencilled in white over the top. The stencils are huge and often multiple boards taped together to ensure that the logo is complete.

There were a few crossing points through the barriers so I could go on either side of the road at that point. I took a picture of the 'house' I had been a guest in on stage 6's finish. Three of them are built at each stage finish and are huge. The commentators have their own 'houses' set up nearer the finish line. Most of the major TV companies are set up in one of the many 'boxes' built into them.

Stade Geoffroy Guichard, the home of St Etienne FC covers a huge area. Around the outside of the stadium there are multiple carparks, several all-weather training pitches, Hockey pitches, an athletics track, tennis courts, and a second football stadium! Loads of space for everything the tour needed to park up somewhere at the finish.

I went to the Zone Technique that was in one of the carparks plus one of their practice pitches at the side of the Stade Geoffroy Guichard. Even they could not cover the entire grounds, but they still came close! The tour diverted all the race vehicles off the race route and into the Clubs grounds so they could be driven past the finish and into one of the secondary carparks, or to the enormous road blocked off for the buses, or in the case of the Caravan, behind the stadium where they all parked up for the night.

I walked back out along the race route from the finish line to find the place I wanted to watch from. I went just over a kilometre. The Flamme Rouge was already up. Just past this the race route ran down a steep hill towards a roundabout which the race had decided was too dangerous with the speeds they would be going at that point. They just cut the roundabout in half, dug it all up and tarmacked over it!! Several Bollards had also had the same treatment. I assume they will put them back before they leave.

I decided to aim for the 500 m to go point to watch the race later. Nice wide road, slight bend, great view. And less people would be there as they were already queuing up by the finish line and they still had 6 or 7 hours to wait for the race to arrive.

As I was still tired, the trams were free and frequent, I decided to go back to the hotel and have a Nana nap! The heat here is getting to me a bit as well so thought it was a good idea! I used the time to sort out my suitcase as it was all over the place!

I got back to the race about 3 pm and met up with Emma. We went over to the buses which had arrived from the start by then to say hi as usual. These were all parked beyond the finish line on the very wide road waiting for the riders at the end of the race. I spoke to Dave Brailsford for a while this time, he had just come back from a 30 kilometre ride. He lived in St Etienne for 3 years so knows the area very well. George came out of the bus to say hi too.

We then walked through the Stadium grounds, to re-join the race route after the 350 metres to go point and walked out to the 500 metres to go point which was a perfect place to watch the race come past. The road was straight, but the barriers had to filter the riders onto the right hand side of the route as the road narrowed just past where we were standing. As such, we could see straight down the road as the riders rode straight at us! We had a great view of De Gendt staying away and winning the stage. Pinot and Alaphilippe were chasing him hard but failed to catch him. The rest of the GC men came in next with some of the sprinters. Awesome. I took a fairly good video of the whole thing as well even though I was still just pointing without looking!

The rest of the riders came in over about the next 15 minutes and I stayed to watch and cheer them all home. No bunch sprint so all those waiting at the finish line had nothing special to watch. Another reason I don't like sprint finishes as they are not guaranteed.

On the way back towards the Tram, we just walked into the Zone Technique! This is usually impossible, but it is the second time I have done this now. I spotted David Millar and Ned Boulting from ITV. All the miles of cabling all over the ground, the huge houses built by each TV network, the NBC house with its interview place on the roof, the giant Eurosport building, loads of stuff and we just wandered round it all. They had a proper toilet bloc too, rather than the Portaloo's scattered along the rest of the route. Very welcome sight!

By this time, most of the crowds had gone so it was easy to get on a tram back to the city centre.

We got off the tram in a lovely square with restaurants all round it. We stopped at the first one we came to and had a drink as it was so hot today. I had a very cold beer which barely touched the sides as it went down! Next, we wandered all-round the outside till we found a lovely Italian place to eat. We sat outside on one of the many tables they had. The food was fabulous. I even took pictures of it! I had a fish salad with Red mullet, prawns, squid, clams, etc, etc. Followed by a banana split! Not had one of those in years!

Hints and tips.

Be prepared for stress, pushing and shoving, large crowds, and an exceptionally long wait! The further you are from the finish line, the better your experience will be.

If you are on the outside of any bend, you will get a better view as the riders will be on the inside of any bend.

49

If you can stay in the finish town, then that is a good option, if not then aim to park in retail parks. It is convenient, and typically easy to get away afterwards. Trains are also a good option here as most sprint finish towns seem to have stations.

If you need to decide between seeing a sprint finish and seeing something else on the stage like a hill, or a beauty spot, then I would choose anything over a sprint finish! Just my opinion though!

Time Trials

I love the Time Trials, both Team (TTT) and individual (ITT). You can get an amazing experience from just about anywhere on a TT. The starts are good as you can still get close to the teams and the riders and the Paddock d'Equipes is rarely behind barriers! Also, it is a good place to see the impressive TT bikes! They are worth the effort just to see them even though they seem smaller than the normal bikes!

Anywhere along the route you will get to see each individual rider come past for several hours! And twice if you are early enough to watch the recons. It is not all over in seconds. If you find the right spot, a long straight road somewhere, then you will see them for ages as well. This goes double for the TTT. A corner can be good too if you want to see them slow down, corner fast then speed back up again. You could even change your viewing place as you have time.

The finishes I have not done. Too many people, cannot see much except the timing gantry, and the riders leave immediately after they get off the bikes and are usually driven straight back to the start! Also, for TTT's they will be down to just five riders so you cannot get the full impact of the eight man teams riding towards you at full speed. But you might like it there! My friend Emma tried this once, failed to get anywhere near the race at all and ended up watching the whole thing on TV back in her hotel room!

Friday, 19th July 2019. ITT. Pau to Pau

I love watching the ITT and the bonus for today is that the ladies will be racing five laps of the same course first for this year's version of La Course. As such I am planning to get to the midpoint of the circuit nice and early so I can watch everything!

The place I am staying is awesome! It is a Gite that is a fully working farm which owns some of the white cows you see all over the Pyrenees. The property was based around a central courtyard and consisted of the main house, a converted barn with ten guest suites, a walled vegetable garden and a new barn where the host cured his own meat. The best bit was they provided an evening meal which was eaten with the family and was you eat what you are given! The meal and the company the night before (my second night there) had been exceptional!

A group of ten lads from a Portuguese Cycling Club had arrived in a minibus with a large trailer holding all their bikes! They had driven all day to get there from Lisbon. They planned to stay at the Farm for two nights. Thomas from Austria was still there from the night before as well. He had been off cycling up two high mountains that day but not on the race route. The hosts daughter and granddaughter were also there for dinner that night, so it was a pretty full house!

Again, we all ate together but we started a bit late waiting for the Portuguese! It was a very warm evening on the edge of the Pyrenees, so the table was set up outside under a barn roof. There was a huge BBQ there as well. We all sat down about 8.30 talking a huge mixture of languages! It was awesome! We again started the meal with the Home Cured Meats with the Sangria. The Portuguese added in some of their own local wine which they insisted we all had too. The next course was Confit Duck with jacket potatoes. Again, it was lovely and came with more wine from France and Portugal! Next was the usual Lettuce course followed by a Lemon Tart on Puff Pastry. It was such a great evening, and I loved every minute of it! We finally finished the meal just after midnight! The Portuguese lads invited Thomas and I to join them on their ride from the farm to the ITT course the next day, but I had had way too much to drink, they were all better cyclists than me, and they were going much further and faster that I could keep up with, so I declined. Thomas did agree to go with them though. I headed to my room, up the way too steep stairs carefully, drank a gallon of water and passed out! I still expected to be hung over the next morning! This whole trip is about people, and I just love it!

It is now extremely hot in France! I spent all day under my brolly and any trees I could get near, and I still cooked. But it was still an enjoyable day! Breakfast was the same very bready one but that was fine. I was ready by 8 am as usual and I had no hangover! Bonus. (and a bit of a surprise to be honest!)

I set off in my car and drove the short distance to the midpoint of the ITT course. This was also the course that the ladies would race on before the men started and I wanted to watch them as well. I found a good place to leave the car. A farmer had opened his field for any cars or campervans, and he did not even charge us! I then set off walking along the route to find a good place to watch from. I found a point where the route came round a corner onto a short downhill section, then turned a hairpin bend and set off on a level piece of ground towards a hill in the distance. I could see them from the start of the downhill bit, right round the hairpin bend, then get up to speed along the flat bit and then finally climb the hill in the distance! Excellent view. There were few others there as it was quite a hike from the nearest parking place.

First up were the ladies and they were Impressive! Their race was a total of five laps of the men's ITT course, so I was able to see them come round five times! Seeing them snake along this small twisty road at full speed was great. By the fifth time past, they were all strung out as the race had split to pieces. I took loads of pictures and videos of them, most of which came out with riders in them!

I had walked to my vantage point, so I was able to carry loads of food and water to last me the entire day. And my brolly obviously as it was so hot! There were four large houses opposite me, and they set up camps on their driveways as the races began to come past. One even started selling cold drinks! As I was on my own for most of the day, one family let me use their loo so that helped!

Next the men started coming round on their ITT recognisance rides. Not race pace but still incredibly fast! And interesting. The hairpin bend was very sharp. The riders going for the win, or the GC took a lot of notice of this corner, some even doing it a couple of times. Fast downhill, break hard to an almost halt, then power away towards the hill.

After that they came past again at race speed! Which was so fast! I could see them break for the hairpin, get up to speed along the straight and then start to climb the hill. I did take some pictures but mostly I just watched as it was fascinating! The side on view of them getting back up to speed was spectacular! Amazing view of everything and there was someone coming past every minute or so. Lovely way to spend the day if you are prepared to wait all day, which I am! And you take your own shade with you! No way I could have stayed out in the full sun all day otherwise.

One thing I did notice as I was so close to the riders' coming past is the noise. The bikes with full disc wheels make this strange humming sound. I cannot describe it in words, but it is very noticeable. And the bikes! Wow. So sleek, so small! And so fast!

Then it was pack up again and head back to the Farm! The guys had also had a wonderful time watching the races but had ended up cycling 130 kilometres! Way too far for me as I did not need to and probably could not anyway! They had been discussing dinner with the hosts as they had been sent off from home with loads of food to prepare by their wives. The result was that we had a mix and match meal of the Hosts food and the Portuguese food. It was amazing! We ended up having about six courses with a different wine with each one!

The starter was the usual meats supplemented with fish and mashed potato balls, some sort of pastry triangles, melon, and a few other nibble bits that I had no idea what they were! Translations failed here. Sangria and or wine with that.

Next the host fired up the giant BBQ and cooked these amazing pork steaks which were served with huge grilled tomatoes. We then had a course from the Portuguese of a sort of risotto which was great. Had that with the lettuce and more choices of wine.

They then produced this flagon of sparkling wine! Some sort of Rose in a giant Demijohn! We had that with some more Portuguese delicacies.

Finally finished the meal with a pudding which I could not eat and some Portuguese sweets which I did try. Plus, more wine and a digestif! It was 2 in the morning before I got up to bed and I was supposed to be cycling up the Tourmalet the next day! (Failed!)

Monday, 8th July 2018. TTT. Cholet to Cholet.

I love watching the TTT. The first one I watched in 2015 had nine man teams. The sight of nine riders lined out going full speed was superb. Unfortunately, the teams are down to eight now, but it is still awesome.

My plan for this year was to go to the 12.5 kilometre to go point which I expected to be empty as it really is miles from anywhere, but it was packed. At 10 in the morning!

I had studied the route before leaving the UK, with the race route starting and finishing in the same town. I knew which side of the race route I needed to be so I would be able to get my car back to wherever I wanted once the race had finished. If you need to cross the race route at any time, it will still be closed to cars hours after the finish. I parked in a field off a side road leading to the race route and under a tree which was handy. The car park was just a farmer's field, and it was going to be difficult to get out of later, but I was in no rush.

Most of the road of the race route was lined with Campervans along the north side of the road, nose to tail. My plan was to watch from the south side so I could get some shade from the trees. The road itself was long and very straight with a 2 kilometre downhill followed by a 2 kilometre uphill. I was stationed at the mid-point of this 4 kilometre stretch, in between the two hills. There was a traffic island right here with a gendarme keeping everyone off it. That helped otherwise you are too close to the riders as they come past, and you miss such a lot.

I arrived at around 10 with the riders due to start coming past for the race at 3.30. I set up my 'camp' on the grass verge with my picnic mat that folds down to the size of a mobile phone! I also have a blow up 'triangle' to use as a back rest which is comfortable and folds up small enough to pack in my rucksack easily. Also had my Yorkshire flag. The heat here is dreadful and I have been getting dehydrated so I walked rather than cycled from my car so I could carry a separate bag full of liquids. I am not steady enough on my bike to balance a bag of heavy liquids and still cycle. I had five litres with me today (which was heavy) but I drank all but one half litre bottle and felt fine all day. I am still dehydrated but it is getting better. I also took my book as I knew there would be down time between the Caravan and the race.

I took enough food for all day, my SheWee and my brolly. The trees did not provide much in the way of shade, but they did provide some which was good. I spent most of the day talking with a lovely French family camping next to me. The wife was seriously ill unfortunately but she managed to remain for the entire day. She seemed to enjoy it. They had a farm just the other side of the trees, so they were able to come and go as they pleased which I am sure helped.

So, the recons started with team Astana who came through about an hour before anybody else! No idea why. I also somehow never saw team Movistar do a recon at all. Strange. Might have fallen asleep? Or maybe they did not do a recon which could be why they were so bad. It is great to see the riders come through slower on the Recon and then race pace later. Got a few pictures but my battery died on my phone. It is just not lasting at all now. My son let me know some actions to take to make the battery last a bit longer each day so should get better from now onwards. Still, it is great to watch without trying to photo as well. The experience is amazing without being side tracked and you can always watch on TV later to see what happened.

As they are going a bit slower on the recons, you also get to see the differences in Size and Shape between the riders who specialise in various aspects of professional cycling. Not sure why it looks so obvious on TT bikes, but the larger, heavier sprinters thunder down the road whereas the CG riders are mostly smaller and lighter but just as fast. Mitchelton Scott looked funny when they came past in the Recon as Matty Hayman (6ft 4 and 80kg) had

Adam Yates behind him (5ft 4 and 58kg) and it looked like a father and son out for a coffee ride! Movistar (when they came past in the race) were all small GC men and they were poor. Katusha are all Huge (for riders) and they were just as bad! So, size does not seem to impact the TTT result, but it really matters in the sprints or the climbs! Sky, Mitchelton Scott, BMC and Quickstep were all a mix of sizes, and they were the fastest teams.

The caravan came past around 2 pm and I hid under my brolly. However, The Cofidis float threw something that landed in my bag! It turned out to be a lovely Snood thing for use under a cycling helmet. Also got some more Haribo!

For the actual race, I had the most amazing view of the riders coming over the hill in formation and then all the way down to my position before they headed off uphill. I could not see so much of them going uphill as they are followed by at least four cars and often a few motorbikes as well! I had my Binoculars with me so could see them well. It is an awesome sight seeing these riders racing along at 80 kph plus all in a line.

I was able to watch the race from 3.30 till 5.20. It was simply great! The sight of the teams coming over the hill at full speed, all lined out one behind the other is just fantastic. I loved every minute of it.

I then packed up and walked back up the hill to the car. I met two people wearing Holmfirth Strip! That's in Yorkshire where I live! They were at their first stage of the tour and had also loved it. It is such a small world!

Wednesday 30th June 2021. ITT. Change to Laval.

Emma was with me again today and my plan was to arrive in Change where I was staying, just next to Laval, where Emma was staying, the day before the race. That would give me all day for the ITT. From Vitre where we watched the intermediate sprint was only 40 minutes so easy for me.

I had to drop Emma off near the centre of Laval, as close as I could get to her Hotel with the one way system and the tour closing lots of the streets! I also wanted to avoid a massive junction at all costs as it was plain scary! Anyway, I managed it ok, dropped Emma off and found the Manoir I was staying at on the second attempt. Huge house behind electric gates. It was a restored mini castle with wood everywhere, and stone flags on all the ground floors. My room was in one of the turrets. I had the whole floor to myself with a large bedroom, a separate loo, and a large bathroom.

I had booked an evening meal here but that was some sort of mistake as none was on offer. It meant I had to go out and buy something to eat which can be a huge problem in France as everywhere shuts so early. I had plenty of time today though as it was only just after 4.30 pm.

I wanted to have a look round the start area of the ITT for the following day which was less than 50 metres away. There was a huge park opposite the Manoir, on which the tour and the town had set up a massive fan park with lots of local stall holders and the usual tour booths. The tour was also beginning to set up the barriers along the roads for the teams and the start box, and the first 2 kilometres of the actual race route. The start town was small, but it did have an excellent Delicatessen, so I bought some tea from there to eat back in my room after a nice long soak in the large bath.

The bed was comfortable, and I slept well which helps. Breakfast was served downstairs in a huge kitchen / diner on a massive solid oak table fit for a castle. Each person had their own breakfast at their place at the table, consisting of some bread products, cakes, bananas, yogurts, tea, coffee, and cereals. I was able to take some of this for my lunch as it would only have been thrown away and was too much for one person.

I had a clicker key for the electric gate so I could come and go as I pleased which was so easy. I also had a front door key and a room key with big brass key fobs, both of which were too heavy to carry round all day. I left those in the car.

I love watching the ITT. They are my favourite stages to watch after the TTT! I did not need to drive anywhere at all today which was a bonus.

I walked through the park and round the tour village, which was quite busy even this early in the morning. I did not find anything I wanted to buy though although I did try some of the local cheeses. I love cheese! Next, I headed to where I knew the buses would be parking shortly and waited there to see who would be where. INEOS arrived early as Luke was Lantern Rouge at that point (rider in last place) and would be first down the start ramp. They were with a couple of other teams in a small car park off to one side. It was easy to walk along the grass at the edge of this car park, so I was able to speak to quite a few people from there.

ITT starts are far more relaxed for everyone except the riders and DS's, so I was able to have a long chat with Rod today. In fact, it was a proper old chin wag! We ranged over so many subjects from schools, to weight, to pandemic stories, and through the issues caused for him specifically and generally by Brexit. The 90 day entry visa was the biggest issue at that time and would only get worse!

I also had a bit of a chat with George about not very much really. Just general stuff. Was such a nice relaxing chat between friends.

Israel Start-up Nation team had parked halfway round a roundabout, and I managed to accost Gary Blem, Froomey's Mechanic. He was quite willing to have a good chat which was so nice. We talked about his move from INEOS, how ISN was a much more relaxed and friendly team, how he was enjoying the new challenge and change of scenery, about stage 19 of the Giro, Froomey's crash (he was in the following car for both of these), Froomey's crash on stage 1, what Gary would be doing that day and what he would be doing over the next few stages. I let him know some of my plans and asked if he would wave if he saw me which he said he would do. Lovely man.

Froome was also going to be an early starter, so I waited to watch him ride off on his recon. He has spoken to me several times over the years and today was no exception. Such a nice man. Others were also beginning to set off for recon rides from all the other teams, so I had great views of many of them while they are still relaxed. I missed Luke Rowe, but I did see Geraint Thomas, Pogacar, Roglic, Bardet, Valverde, and many others. I saw most of them come back too! The whole area of the paddock was along a small road, round a roundabout, and then across a bridge. This meant that it was easy to get close to everything without having to get inside the barriers. I had a fun time this morning.

I then went round a lot of the teams to take as many pictures of bikes, buses, mechanics trucks, and cars as I could for the Yorkshire Lasses to try and show just how much stuff is needed for eight riders for one ITT!

Next, I wandered towards the start and past the start 'box' with the start ramp. Along a wall there were all the magnetic signs with each rider's surname on, lined up in order of departure, ready to be stuck to the front of the car that would follow them along the route. Often, reading this is the only way to know who has just gone past!

My plan was to walk along the race route for about 2 kilometres to a straight piece of road, camp on the grass and watch everyone come past. The walk was slightly uphill at first, then as the route headed out of town there was a roundabout followed by a straight section of road that went steeply downhill then back uphill and I decided to set up camp at the top of the uphill section. From here I could see all the way back to the roundabout and watch the riders as they rounded the next corner. There was a small grass verge with a culvert behind it that had posts at intervals to warn drivers of the drop off. I set up my picnic mat, flag, bag etc so I could lean against one of these posts. That was quite comfortable for a long wait.

On the way to my camping spot, I walked past a local group who had set up a BBQ in a car park near the roundabout. I decided to buy some extra food for lunch from here. I got a foot long sausage, some chips, and a beer for next to nothing which was surprisingly tasty although difficult to carry to my campsite!

I got a bit wet too as the rain started as soon as I arrived at my campsite. I naturally had my Brolly, so it was not a problem and better than being too hot. I watched everyone come past and took some videos and some photos, and really enjoyed my day. It was just a shame that talking to others is not possible due to Covid restrictions, but I was still there so that was fine. Watching the riders individually is different from all in a bunch. You can see the differences in sizes, effort, technique, speed, everything. It is fun to try and work out who the next rider is before they get close enough to read the name on the car behind just from the size and shape! And, exceedingly difficult. The team colours help narrowing it down though but there is little time to get it right before they are past and gone.

Last rider came past, I packed up and wandered back towards the town, which was still packed. There was a huge TV screen in the middle of the town, so I watched the last riders come through the finish line in Laval on that before heading to the Deli to pick up something for tea. Back at the Manoir, the hostess came straight up and said that one of the riders had spent quite some time in her front room! She had a picture. It was obviously Mattieu Van der Poel! In her front room! Wow.

Hints and tips.

Take the time to enjoy the whole experience, from the recons to the actual race. It is worth it.

Anywhere you watch from will be worth it. I have found that from the starts you can also see them all racing with just a little effort and a short walk or cycle!

I have not done the end of an ITT or a TTT and I am not looking to either.

The race route will be shut all day from at least 6 am, until several hours after the race has finished, so planning your approach and leaving routes is essential.

Car parking is often ok at starts as the organisers seem to plan that with fields opened as car parks within a reasonable walking distance. Mid points are also easy, just pick a road to park on. Just make sure you are on the right side of the race route to get away though as the roads remain closed for ages after the race has finished.

It is often the case that the start and finish towns are small for Time Trials, so public transport can be difficult to get to either of them. And they will not take you to a mid-point. Cycling from the nearest train station is realistically your only option.

Finishes are not easy to get to as the roads are all closed around the finish towns, and on all the roads back to the start town, so the teams and officials can use nearby roads to get back to the start.

A bike is handy. It will make finding the perfect spot to watch from easier as you can go further, faster but the race route will probably be restricted access so you will need to check the route and where you intend to go to find out if you will need one.

Cobbles

How to describe the Cobbles? Horrendous is the first word that springs to mind! The stones that make up these cobbled stretches are the size and shape of Farmhouse loaves of bread. And they have been in the ground for hundreds of years. They are not even close to flat and level. The only way to understand what they are like is to take a bike and ride them for yourselves.

Tuesday 7th July 2015. Finish in Cambrai.

I am in France, on my own, at the Tour de France, and I am feeling excited, plus a bit nervous and, by the time I get into Cambrai, totally bewildered.

I had been looking at as many bike races on TV as I could over the preceding few months trying to get a feel for what to expect once I got to France, but the reality of the Tour is off the scale! It's overwhelming.

I had driven from Calais to just south of Cambrai to the Gite I was staying in for the Monday and Tuesday nights, so I would be ready to head into Cambrai as early as possible on Tuesday's race day to see the end of stage 4. Driving in France on the wrong side of the road was fine (except for turning left at T junctions!) and I had eventually found this lovely Gite after only a few wrong turns. It really was in the back of beyond. The owners had converted one of their barns into a bed and breakfast place. I had a huge room with a lovely view out of the window over rolling farmland.

Breakfast was included in the price at the Gite and was excellent. The hosts cooked Eggy Brioche which was lovely, there were cereals, there were cheeses and cooked meats, and at least four different types of bread. The Gite was part of a working farm and the piece de resistance was some fresh picked, pale pink, raspberries which were just fabulous! They were still warm from the morning sun.

Some other people were also at breakfast that morning having arrived late the night before. A group were with Eurosport as reporters or something. I only knew that because of the name plastered all over the side of their car. There was also a couple from Australia. The world comes to France in July. They were over to see the Tour, but to also visit the Somme where their ancestor had fought during the first world war. The whole area of the first stages I was going to see had been heavily impacted by the first world war. Cambrai tourist office tells of miles of underground tunnels all around the area dug during the war.

I somehow, and with quite a few wrong turnings, managed to get back to Cambrai, and to the carpark I had identified using Google Maps before I left for France, as a good place to leave the car. It was part of a retail park so had plenty of parking available if you were OK with a 2 kilometre walk to the town centre. That was fine by me! I walked into the centre of Cambrai which is very quaint and pretty with large plaza's, grand old buildings, and parks, and it had vanished under a sea of vehicles! The media village had set up in the main carpark and all over the central plaza, and it was huge. There were hundreds of lorries and trailers which had all been extended and opened out into small houses. There was even a 50 ft crane in the middle covered in satellite dishes. The whole area was surrounded by a 6 ft high fence patrolled by guards with guns! Wow!

I walked round what will have been the town square the previous day and it was covered in barriers and banners as the actual finish was along one side of it. The podium was there, the hospitality houses were there, the commentary boxes were there, the whole place was completely transformed overnight. There was even a fold out stand with seating for several hundred people. I had no idea just how huge the logistics behind the race were and it was fascinating. Beware, I am a bit of a planner at heart, and I loved this massive logistical puzzle.

I followed the barriers down the race route for about 3 kilometres, just so I could see the extent of the barriers and there I found the lorry park for all the vehicles that had brought the miles and miles of barriers off to one side and out of the way of any TV coverage.

There was a 3 kilometre to go banner, and the 'flame rouge' or 1 kilometre to go banner. Giant TV screens were set up along the side of the route in the final kilometre. It was only 11 in the morning with the race not due to arrive until 4.30 at the earliest, and there were people everywhere already. It was impossible to find a spot to watch against the barriers in the final 250 metres, so I decided to find a nice table to sit at in one of the many cafes in the un-barriered part of the main square, have a coffee and just watch everything that was going on. Just chillin'!

On the way to the cafes that lined two sides of the square, I spotted Greg Lemond. He won the Tour de France three times. He was just getting ready to go for a ride before he was due to do his bit on Eurosport. He was lovely. I was amazed that you could just walk up and talk to someone that famous. He let me take his picture as well. The next person I spotted was Chris Boardman. Our first ever cycling Olympic Gold Medallist. He had also worn the Yellow Jersey once. And I just went straight up and spoke to him as well. Lovely man. My confidence it seems has also started to come back as I lost the excess weight I had been struggling with for most of my life. Finally, as I was heading towards a table, I spotted Gary Imlach. He is the anchor man for ITV's Tour Coverage. Another chance to accost a famous person so naturally that is what I did. I was having a ball! I have pictures of all of them just to prove that I did meet them. I even asked Chris if we might be related. It is possible he is an ex cousin in law of some degree or other, but I have never really tried to find out for certain. Suffice to say, my Ex Father in law and Chris look identical when both were 50!

I finally found a good seat right on the edge of a café's patio, got my coffee, and watched for ages. It was fascinating. There were lots of people wandering about dressed in Lycra from various clubs or in their favourite teams' kits. I spoke to a young lad in a GB kit who was going to cycle the route out about 10 kilometres to a section of cobbles. That sounded such a great idea, but I had no bike. Walking 10 kilometres was too far. I spoke to as many people as stood still long enough and were not rude enough to escape! People from all over the world. Everyone had a story to tell as to why they were there, how cycling had helped them, who they supported, what they expected and how much just being there had way exceeded any expectations.

I decided to watch the riders come across the line from just after the finish right next to the base of the stand of seating as I could get a place to watch from there and see a TV screen in the Vittel stand opposite. I had an unobstructed view of the finish presentation podium as well. There was a café just behind my position, so I could get coffee and use their loo! Perfect. I was going to be stood there for several (3!) hours. I started talking to a lovely French couple who were doing the same. They saved my space for me each time I had to leave it for a short pit stop or a caffeine fix.

Oh my God! The Publicity Caravan hove into view. What an astonishing sight that was. There was a giant furry lion being driven down the road, Mickey Mouse was there, a giant orange, even a giant car tyre! I have no idea how many floats there were, but it took ages for them all to pass. It was quite a spectacle. I had no idea they were even part of the Tour. We had had a few floats come past during the race in Yorkshire in 2014, but nothing on this scale. The noise of the music blaring out, the sheer number of people on each float singing and dancing and generally being extremely cheerful, was great. And the stuff being thrown out to the crowds as they passed. Must have been tons of it. The couple beside me told me the caravan had been driving along the entire days route throwing stuff out all day to the crowds on the side of the road. It must have cost a fortune, but it was still great to watch. I had no idea this even happened as it never gets on TV.

Next across the finish line came the team buses. These buses are spectacular all in a convoy with the team colours all over them. Twenty-two of them slowly driving past is just such a remarkable thing to see. It somehow made the race and the fact that I was there seem more real.

Then I had an hour or so to wait for the race to arrive. There was still lots to see though – VIP's arriving, TV crews doing bits to camera at the finish line, the Podium crews doing run throughs, umpteen vehicles arriving along the race route for heaven knows what reason. It was just an amazing experience. The couple I was with at the side of the road had watched several stages over the years and were able to let me know so much of what I was watching in a mixture of my dreadful French and their basic English. The time flew by.

Eventually, the race itself arrived. That stage had been raced over dirt and cobbled roads covered in dust so when the riders arrived it was almost impossible to spot who was who as they were all the same dirty grey / brown colour with very muddy faces! Tony Martin (Time Trial Specialist par excellence) won but I only found that out later. Even Chris Froome in the bright yellow leader's jersey was difficult to spot in all the dust-spattered kit. I took loads of pictures and had to wait till I got back to see if I could work out just who I had seen. The pictures seemed to clean the riders up a bit and give a false view of just how dirty the riders were. I was in full point and press mode without looking through the view finder as the riders all came past. It is a miracle I managed to get so many good pictures especially the one of Froome.

I was so close! The riders were all right next to me. Some even leant on the barriers I was standing behind. I was totally amazed at just how close you can get to them all. I loved the atmosphere, the drama, the mud-spattered faces, the exhaustion in their body language, everything. I would totally recommend anyone to go over and just see something of the Tour. I had seen my first stage end, and it was so much more than the TV can ever convey.

All the team buses had parked just a bit further up the road but outside the fenced off bit, so you could just walk up to the buses and see the riders doing their cool down rides (except the Sky bus which was surrounded with fans). I got to see my first Billionaire as Oleg Tinkoff was at his bus He is the owner of the Tinkoff Team who Contador rides for. It was fun just wandering around that area. 50 minutes later and they had all gone! Half the barriers had also been dismantled by the time I had walked back to the finish line and the lorries were starting to collect them. The finish gantry was being folded up into its trailer ready to be driven off. The media village was still in full flow with bits to camera and stuff going on. I went back to my table for another coffee and watched the media village begin to be folded up into trailers ready to be driven off to the end of the next stage. The whole thing was a massive example of logistics at work. Being a bit of a geek and definitely a planner, I found this whole thing just so interesting. From watching on TV this whole side of the Tour is invisible. I was so glad I had come over to watch.

I walked back to my car and eventually found the Gite again after some more wrong turns. It was such a hard place to find. I had brought my tea with me and met up with the Australians who had done the same. We all had dinner together in the Gite's lovely garden, discussing the day we had had, what we had seen and just how much fun the day had been. At least we did until a swarm of midges descended and we had to retreat indoors!

Wednesday 6th July 2022. Cobbles. Lille to Wallers-Arenberg.

I was staying in a pretty place the night before the Cobbled stage. The evening meals there were gourmet style and fabulous! There were four white stucco buildings set out round a square grass area with patios, tables and chairs, trees, flower beds, and sunshades. Having a cold beer in this garden before going in for a meal is a lovely way to end a day. I had met Emma at the stage on the Tuesday as the only way to get to the cobbled sections was by car, so I was giving her a lift. It would be her first experience of Cobbles, without a bike as she does not have one.

Breakfast was the usual bready affair, but the egg poacher was perfect! I love eggs for breakfast. Again, I took some stuff for lunch, but I intended to stop at a supermarket near the cobbles to stock up on water, bananas, and anything else I felt like I needed rather than just bread.

From the supermarket, it was only a short drive to the cobbled section I was aiming for. I had checked the route of this stage when the route came out in October to try and find the best pace to see the cobbled sections. There were eleven sectors, starting with sector 11 after 80 kilometres of flat racing, to sector 1 which was only 6 kilometres from the finish line. Sectors 8 and 7 were close enough together to be able to ride both before the race came through but overly complicated to get to by car. Sectors 4 and 3 were also close enough to ride both but were just off the main A23. That is how I chose sectors 4 and 3 to ride this year.

The drive to the place I intended to park should only have taken 40 minutes. Unfortunately, Lille struck again! Every time I have tried driving anywhere near Lille, I have gone wrong. The road signs are dreadful, and the roads are just so confusing. I ended up on the wrong road, going the wrong direction so I came off the autoroute to try and turn round but I was too close to the race start in the centre of Lille! We ended up driving round in circles for about 40 minutes until we found a way out of Lille that was still open. Still going the wrong way but at least from here we could find a way around the city and back towards the road we wanted to be on.

Once back on the right road, it was easy to get to the supermarket I was aiming for to stock up on food and liquids. It was only a 10 kilometre drive from there to where I wanted to get to. Without Emma, I would have cycled the final 10 kilometres to make it easier to get away after the race, but it was still easy to do by car today. I planned to keep driving until I reached the road closures at the start of sector 3, then turn round and park as soon as I could. That went perfectly. I managed to park less than 1 kilometre from the entrance to sector 3, up against a hedge which would provide some shade for the car as the day was going to be hot.

I unpacked my bike from the car and set off to ride the two sectors of cobbles on my plan. I rode sector 3 first as that was the one I thought I would be most likely to watch from. It was also the worst one. I could then abandon riding the second one if I needed to or if any bits fell off me or my bike on the first sector. Both sectors could be ridden as part of a figure of eight with normal roads joining them together. I had parked my car on the middle of the figure 8.

Sector 3 was truly dreadful! I bounced and rattled all the way along the 2.4 kilometres. There is no way to describe what it is like to ride cobbles. You just have to try it for yourself. I loved it! This sector was several long straight sections with right angle bends joining them together. The 'road' had been here forever, was used daily by tractors, and was in a dreadful condition. The sectors are ranked from 1* to 5* with 5* being the worst. This sector was a 3* so what a 5* is like I am not sure I want to find out. But I did it! I got to the end! I was overtaken by some people walking I was going so slowly at points, but I did get there eventually.

The cobble stones on this sector are all roughly the size and shape of a Farmhouse loaf of bread. They might at one time have been laid in straight lines on a level plane but now they are all off set with different size gaps between them. And often missing altogether! Many have sunk into the ground. There is a ridge in the centre that is less worn with deep tyre ruts either side. If you can go fast enough it might be possible to stay on the ridge in the middle. For me, I just could not keep up there! I kept getting thrown off to one side or the other. Riding in the tyre ruts was where the roughest cobbles were. At least I did not crash so that is a result. And nothing fell off my bike either!

I rode back to the car on the main road, then set off towards the start of sector 4. I rode that too. That was quite different.

The first sector was old, well used, and large cobbles. The second sector was flatter, and had obviously been re-laid, but the gaps between the stones was huge! Made them really jarring to ride for again 2.4 kilometres. They were all off set so your front wheel could be on a stone while the back one was in a gap. Seconds later and that was reversed. I did not fall off, but it was close a few times. This was also a 3* sector. The cobbles were different too as they were newer, smaller, squarer, and less rounded. I found this sector harder to ride which seems odd. The shaking here was extreme! But again, no crashes, and nothing fell off me or my bike.

Then it was a short ride back to the car, which was parked at the midpoint of the figure of eight, pick up my ruck sack and days supplies and ride off to find a field on sector 3 to camp out for several hours.

Brolly, SheWee, lots of water, picnic mat, Yorkshire flag, and food all squashed into a small rucksack which is an art in itself. The field I found was on a very straight section with a field of corn on one side and a bit of scrub opposite. I put my bike with the flag over it in the scrub, as far away from the route as possible and set up camp on the edge of the corn field. Flattened a few stalks to make the area big enough and comfortable. It is just a case of sit and wait then.

I tried to take some pictures to show just how bad the cobbled surface was, but it is so hard to convey their awfulness and I am in no way a photographer.

The crowds were huge even that early on. There was a campervan site a few 100 metres up the road from my camp, on a bend, with some Tour De France stalls, and a bar. Parties everywhere. The Publicity Caravan was not allowed along the cobbles, so I avoided that today.

People continued to arrive by bike and on foot all day long. By the time the race arrived, the whole area was rammed. I still had a fairly unobstructed view though as I had picked my spot well. I could see all the way back to the entrance to the sector as that was higher than where I was. I could then see the race go round one right angled corner, along a short straight piece and then round a second right angled corner going the opposite way. Finally, the race came along a very straight 1 kilometre stretch with me watching from the centre of this straight. I could see them coming towards me, past me and then away into the distance. Great view.

As usual, I was not looking through the viewfinder of my phone camera as the rider's past. I did manage to get one of the videos with riders in the middle. Rest were a bit rubbish. Lots of feet in them for some reason.

Watching the riders go so fast over these cobbles is amazing. But the dust! No idea how they manage to continue to breathe. It's the cars all around them that create most of the dust. ASO should leave them all off the cobbles and just let the cyclists ride them. That would be great. Fortunately, there was a bit of wind today and that was blowing from behind me which meant I could still see something of the race as it passed.

The race was scattered all over the place by the time they reached sector 3. The race counts the cobbled sections down from 11 to 1 so 3 was only about 15 kilometres from the finish.

The riders kept coming passed for about 40 minutes. Some riders had obviously come off somewhere judging by the blood and the shredded kit. All of them were filthy!

Most tried to ride on the ridge down the middle of the cobbles and even they made hard work of staying on it. The first rider's past were in a small group but the peloton was in a much larger group, so riders were on both edges as well. That is where most punctures come from. Speed, noise, skill, dust, what a day!

I love watching these sections, but I can also see the point that they should not be part of a grand tour. Is watching the riders bounce all over these sectors worth loosing contenders for the overall race? They have the potential to reduce the enjoyment of the next fifteen stages and the overall race so are they worth the risk? I am not sure but if they are in the race, I will be there watching.

Back to the car, then off to Mons, Belgium. Huge traffic snarl up on the motorway so we went cross country. We would still be driving otherwise! Found the place eventually and what a place. It was modern, like a cube, with the most massive solid oak slice of tree trunk for a table. I took a picture of it because it was beautiful.

The place also kept bees! Several hives in the garden. They also did an evening meal, a get what you are given menu, but I like these the best. Tonight, it was the most amazing burger with Avocado, with chunky chips and a side salad which I would have been happy with as the main meal. It was lovely.

Dessert was honey ice cream, nuts, a honey brittle, with fresh honeycomb and bee pollen. Sat watching their bees while eating in their garden. Fabulous place.

Sunday, 14th July 2018. Cobbles. Arras to Roubaix.

I am staying in Amiens which is a beautiful place. The finish of yesterday's stage was in the town centre and that was brilliant but a story for another day. A bit random I know but staying in the same place as me last night was the British representative for the World Clay Pidgeon Shooting Championships and his manager. It is still all about people for me at the tour. I spoke to the Clay Pidgeon Shooters again this morning at breakfast. They had not been able to see any of the race yesterday, as they had been training nearer to Arras all day. They had seen the aftermath when they got back though and were impressed at just how big the Tour is.

I had already sorted out what I needed to take with me for the day as I knew I was going to be sat in a field for around 4 hours in the baking sun with wind and dust everywhere. I had bought some food to take with me and added to this from Breakfast plus as much liquid as I could get on my bike. I had my Picnic mat, my blow up back support, my Yorkshire flag, my SheWee, and my brolly. That is a lot to get into one backpack.

I left the hotel around 9 am and drove from Amiens to the cobbled sector 14 which took about 2 hours but only because I got well lost on the small back roads! I am sure I drove down the same road at least four times and not all in the same direction either. I had identified a small area of what looked like parkland, off a small road as near the finish of sector 14 as I could get. I needed to park near the finish of the sector as it was a rest day the next day and the tour was relocating all the way to Annecy. A drive of over 800 kilometres! I needed to be as far south on the race route so I could get away easily. I would stop overnight in Dijon as that is way too far to drive in one go for me, especially after sitting in a field in the sun all day.

I found it eventually though and parked up in as much shade as I could. I was about 5 kilometres from the exit point of sector 14 which was easy to ride to along roads that were blocked off and therefore quiet. There were fifteen sectors of cobbles on the stage and each one was counted down towards the finish in Roubaix so sector 14 was the second section they rode over. The sectors are also 'rated' by 1* to 5*, 1* being the smoothest and 5* being extremely unpleasant. The sector I was on was a 2* and it was dreadful.

I left my car on the main road and cycled to the sector. Todays cobbled sector was 1.5 kilometres in length, fairly straight and definitely downhill. I was going to ride the whole sector from the exit to the entrance, so it was also going to be uphill for me at first. Off I went. It was awful, and exhilarating! I bounced and struggled the entire 1.5 kilometres. I managed to not stop once which was a result. I also managed to not fall off either which was extremely lucky! I then rode back to around the mid-point as that was the best place to watch from. I rode VERY SLOWLY as I was now going downhill, and I am not good at downhills. I was also shaken to pieces! My hands hurt the most and they were still painful a few days later. My Bike survived though which was the main worry. I do not have a car following me with spares for bits that might fall off. And I would have no clue what to do with them even if I did! The Cobbles are not like the ones we have in England. They are huge. Each one is about the size of a large loaf of bread, and all rounded just like a loaf. They are not particularly close together either, so you sort of bounce from one stone to the next. Then if you miss a stone, it throws you into the gap between them and tries to tip you off. I am so glad I gave this a go though as the TV gives you no clue as to what it is like. I was on a 2* sector so I cannot imagine what a 5* was like.

Around the middle of the sector, I set up my usual camp in a field of harvested Barley. They had left the straw in lines which made it easy to use as a soft cushion. I banked up the straw, put my mat over it, blew up my back rest, set up my brolly to give some shade and settled down to wait the 4 hours for the race to arrive. I spoke to a lovely elderly French couple who had parked their car in the middle of the field the day before so they could use it to sit down in. They could not sit on the ground so their planning worked well for them. That was when I realised I had left my phone in the car!

I asked the French couple to keep an eye on my camp and set off back to the car. 0.8 kilometres of cobbles and then 5 kilometres to the car. I picked up my phone, then rode back to my campsite. 1.6 kilometres further than I had planned to ride on the cobbles. Not forgotten my phone since though!

The caravan did not come down the cobbled sectors, so I missed that today. It did mean I could not get any extra liquids which was a shame, but the cobbles are just too bad and too narrow for lorries.

It was so hot! And the dust! It was dreadful especially every time a vehicle went past. I was covered in a thick layer of it by the time the race had gone past. The race itself was amazing. Watching them go past at around 25 to 30 miles per hour over that terrain was impressive.

And the noise! Bikes rattling, shouts, and hordes of cars whizzing past after each group of cyclists went by. The race was in bits by then with riders scattered all over the place. Meant I could see them quite clearly as they tended to be all lined out on the centre of the road. There was too much dust to be able to spot individual riders though, but it was possible to see teams if they were all still together.

I packed up my camp and rode back to my car and drove the 300 kilometres to Dijon where I am staying tonight. It is a place I have stayed before which is nice. It was hot again today. Sat in a field under an umbrella for 4 hours in 32 degree heat is not that pleasant but way better than not having an umbrella! It was humid as well today and with the dust, that stuck to me everywhere. But as I drove south, the clouds bubbled up and it started to rain. The temperature dropped rapidly to around 22 degrees. Its back up to 25 degrees now but so nice.

I have just had a lovely meal here of four courses with lots of fresh veg and salad as side dishes. They do the Cheese course before the dessert course which is nice as I love the local cheeses. I can take or leave the dessert then.

It took ages to get all the dust off when I arrived though, and I will need to do some washing asap as I have again run out of clothes.

On a side note, there was no traffic at all (as in not a soul anywhere!) as I approached my hotel. That was around 6.30 local time which coincided with a certain cup final. There are still cars driving round now though, blowing their horns so I know who had won before I even logged on to check! And several lots of Fireworks have gone up even though it is still raining. I was still able to sleep that night as I was exhausted.

Hints and tips.

If there is a chance to go to a cobbled sector, then make sure you go with a bike! Walking is possible but the challenge of riding the cobbles is everything.

Early sectors will have less people on them, later ones will be packed. Decide on what you want to experience before picking the sector to watch from.

Be prepared to wait for the race to arrive. Getting there early is always best in my opinion although people will still be arriving as the race arrives!

Wait for all the riders and the broom wagon to pass before packing up and leaving. What is the point of sitting in a field for hours waiting for a race to arrive and then leaving before seeing all the riders? You will be surprised how many people do though.

Most sectors are in the middle of nowhere. Access is by car, then bike or walk. Planning is needed here to ensure that you do not cross the race route with your car, either on arrival or leaving as the road will be shut.

Rest Days

These take two different forms. The first is to enable the entire tour to relocate to a different part of Europe. The riders will fly, but everyone else will have to drive, including me. France is a big country so be prepared for a long drive. I have not added any examples of this type of rest day as they are a bit boring to be honest.

The second type of rest days are awesome! These are where the end of the stage before the rest day is either the same place or close to the start of the stage after the rest day. As such, the rest day usually covers at least 3 days rather than just one. I have loads of examples of these and have selected three to share with you.

Rest day in Andorra Viella, 2016.

The stage before the rest day ended up the HC climb of Arcalis. The teams would then all stay in and around the main town in Andorra with the start after the rest day from the town centre. I stayed in a huge five star hotel in the centre of Andorra Viella for three nights. It was the most expensive place I stayed this tour. The impact to my budget meant I had to stay in small, less expensive places for the rest of the tour.

My plan meant that I arrived in Andorra the night before the stage was due to finish on Arcalis but as Arcalis was a step too far for me in 2016, I planned to try and get up the Côte de la Comella, a 4.2-kilometre-long climb at 8.2%, category 2 instead. I could get there from the hotel as it was only 3 kilometres to the base of the climb, and that was downhill on the main road. I would have to cycle backup it on the way home, but it was probably the flattest road in the whole of Andorra at only around 5%! The Cote de la Comella was only a short climb, but it looked steep. I could see the mountain from the hotel, and it seemed to be vertical. Anyway, I could always walk.

I slept well in a comfortable bed in a quiet, air-conditioned room. I was up early as usual and went down for breakfast. There was an enormous variety of food on offer here. Definitely a 5-star breakfast with fresh pineapple, peaches, and apricots, eggs, poached, fried, boiled, scrambled or an omelette, tomatoes, sausages, smoked salmon, cheeses, many different breads, cereals, everything you can think of, and it was there. I could also order a full English Fried Breakfast if I really wanted to which to be honest I did not. There were also six different fresh squeezed juices. I picked up lunch from here as there was no way I could better this food anywhere else.

I had loads of time that morning as the race was not due to arrive on the Category 2 climb until around 4.30 ish so I went down to the lobby / lounge for a coffee and in walked some staff from the IAM Cycling team! This World Tour team is staying in this hotel for the next two nights. This is going to be fun.

20 mins later and two personnel from Team Sky walked in! They are staying in this hotel as well for 2 nights! OMG! I could not believe my luck. The two Team Sky guys were transporting what looked like fold up tables and turned out to be the massage tables. They also had mattresses and other stuff to carry in. I went straight up to both, and they stopped to talk to me for ages. They were so friendly. And they were just the advanced guard. Shortly afterwards, two Sky trucks parked in the carpark opposite (Kitchen truck and a Mechanics truck), followed by more vans, more trucks and the biggest 16-wheel campervan I have ever seen! IAM cycling also started to have vehicles arrive and try and squeeze into the same carpark. When the Pro Continental team (one step below the World Tour Teams) of Fortuneo - Vitel Concept also turned up to stay in the same hotel I realised

that this was going to be a fun place to watch as they tried to squeeze everything into the way too small carpark. They had been allocated around one-third of the parking area, but they soon started to move the barrier tape over, so they took up over half of it. Some cars already parked there got a bit boxed in.

I had to get up the category 2 climb today, so I needed to get on with it! I left the hotel around 1 pm and set off. The downhill was easy but as soon as I turned left at the foot of the climb the road became a wall! I managed less than 200 metres before I had to stop. It was like this all the way up. Some places were just so steep I knew I could not even ride down them let alone up! I struggled onwards though, and I got to the top eventually. On the way, I passed an Ipswich Town Football Club flag attached to a few trees! The flags owners were there on holiday so had come out to see what all the fuss was about. I passed lots more people in Sky kits but again they were mostly Spanish. I thought they might be support for Mikkel Landa, but they were all there for Froome.

On one of the many hairpin bends, there was what looked like some sort of park or at least less steep grassy area. There were several parties going on here. There were what looked like giant BBQs built on Railway Sleepers with metal gates as the grills. Lots of food being cooked on these which they were most willing to share with a random English woman pushing a bike up a very steep hill! Did I mention before that the whole route was one giant party? Because that is exactly what it was. I was having a ball!

At the top of the climb, I again took some pictures of my bike against the summit banner just to prove that I had climbed to the top of my second mountain in this year's Tour. Two mountains. The feeling I get even now writing about it, when I remember just what I achieved, is immense.

The weather stayed dry where I was all day, unlike on Arcalis. They had apocalyptic conditions with rain, thunder, lightning, and hail stones the size of golf balls. After getting to the top of La Comella, I came back down (Very gingerly!) to around the midpoint of the climb where there was a straight road between two hairpin bends. The edges of the road dropped straight down a tree lined slope / cliff on one side and went up a sheer rocky cliff on the other. I stayed on the rocky cliff side behind a deep channel cut along the edges of the road to take away the rain. I had a perfect view and got some fairly good pictures of the race when it came by. Unfortunately, when the caravan came past, I was standing by myself, and I got loads and loads of stuff thrown at me. I must have had around 40 Madeleines for a start! I tried to give some of these away to people still walking up. Fortunately, I had one of the McCain carrier bags thrown at me (I got several in fact plus some other bags as well) which I was able to fill up with all the stuff thrown my way. I cannot leave it on a mountain side as it is littering, and I just will not do that. The bag was full, and I had to try and get it all back down on my bike somehow. I ended up with it on my right shoulder and resting on the cross bar which made me very unstable! I put most of the stuff in various litter bins when I got back to the main road. And I was right, in some places I could not cycle down as the brakes just could not be held tight enough. Others managed it but not me.

Back at the hotel after a shower and change to normal clothes, I was ready to sit down in the lobby with a coffee to await the riders. First though I took some pictures from my room window of the giant game of Tetrus being played with team vehicles in the carpark down below. It was so funny. Sky had the far side of the car park, IAM had the near side and Fortuneo had the bit by the entrance and anywhere they could squeeze a vehicle between the two World Tour teams' vehicles.

Most of the riders were dropped off by car rather than by the buses which meant they arrived in dribs and drabs. I was able to speak to Froome, Rowe, Kiriyenka, Nieve, all of them. They are all just so approachable. And I said hi to lots of the IAM cycling and Fortuneo riders although I had no idea who most of them were. One was Mattias Frank but no idea which one.

Watching Froome walk along is quite funny as he can only take a few steps before he must stop for another Selfie or Autograph. And he always stops. He seems to have the patience of a saint.

I watched them all arrive and head off to their rooms and the massage tables etc, then went outside to see what was going on there. The IAM Cycling bus had arrived via the one-way system at a button roundabout and got stuck on it! It was so funny. There were vehicles everywhere. Cars, Trucks, vans, even Fortuneo - Vitel Concept, the Pro Continental team, had a kitchen truck and a chef. I went around to count the Sky vehicles and there were –

6 cars

1 Ford Mustang

2 transit vans

1 Kitchen truck

1 mechanic's truck

1 trailer full of washing machines and tumble driers.

1 Freezer van

1 monster Campervan the same size as the team bus!

1 Team bus

1 Generator truck

2 Shopping trolleys used to ferry round hundreds of bottles of water from Supermarkets to the Hotel Freezers!

Heaven only knows how many bikes!

Both IAM Cycling and Fortuneo - Vitel Concept had similar numbers and types of vehicles. The logistics of moving these all around France is fascinating. And I wondered what they all did. How much stuff do nine riders need? I had all the rest day to try and find out.

The team staff were all busy washing everything in sight. Eventually the Sky riders came back out and went over to their Kitchen truck which was also their personal dining room.

Again, Froome took ages to get across to the truck as he stopped for every selfie and autograph. The Spanish here absolutely Love him.

I spoke to everyone who stood still long enough. The two Team Sky guys who had been the first to arrive were lovely. One worked for Ford and the other worked for Sky Media. But they still moved equipment around for the team. No one is exempt from that. They stopped and spoke with me several times and I got loads of info from them regarding the logistics side of things. And a few Sky caps for the Grandkids. And a Sky Key Ring for me.

Once the riders had gone to the dining truck, I had to find something for me to eat too. The IAM cycling team did not have a Kitchen Truck or a mobile dining room but took over the Hotels facilities and some of the dining space. There was also all the staff from all three teams eating in the main restaurant which was rammed. No chance I could get in. So, I headed out into the town. It is a bit of a strange town centre really. There were loads of nice places to eat but the rest of the shops were all selling high-end duty-free stuff. Or Hotels. Nothing at all seemed to be Andorran. And it all seemed to have been built recently. It is set in the most amazing setting though in a sort of bowl surrounded by towering mountains. As you go out of the centre and up the sides of the 'bowl' you could see that the architecture changed and became more alpine and more what I expect is traditional Andorran.

After another excellent breakfast the following morning, I set up at a table at the side of the lobby with my laptop, camera and a coffee and watched everyone milling about. There were twenty-seven very skinny guys in Lycra, (no idea who half of them were!), lots of team staff rushing all over the place, and loads of fans everywhere. There were also a lot of Journalists hovering about as well including the ITV 4 crew. I spoke to Ned Boulting for a short while. He was waiting for the rest day conference / interview with Froome which was originally going to be at the Hotel but for some reason had been moved to a different venue that the riders would cycle to around 10.30 ish before heading out on their rest day rides.

I spoke with Rod Ellingworth (Head of Performance at Team Sky) for ages. What a nice man. He was really interested in what I had to say so I told him how Chris Froome had saved my life. How much weight I had lost. How much fun I was having following the Tour. Loads of stuff. He was just so easy to talk to. He told me some bits about how everything ran behind the scenes such as the moving from hotel to hotel each day and what his role was on race days. He was driving the Mustang ahead of the race to check out weather conditions, road conditions, feeding logistics, road pinch points, etc. Anything that could impact the riders that was not obvious from the road book.

I watched Froome try and get out of the hotel passed all the waiting fans again. Still three paces seemed to be the maximum he could manage in a row before having to stop. He did tend to avoid Journalists though and I do not blame him. They are dreadful and treat him with little or no respect at all. Whereas the Spanish absolutely love him! Froome carries his own pen with him for all the autograph hunters.

I followed everyone outside to see what was going on and to watch the riders leave for their days ride. The whole car park was a hive of activity with bikes being 'fettled' or washed, cars being cleaned, washing being done, cooking, shopping, unpacking and re packing, it was busy in all three camps. One thing that is done on a rest day is to fill every vehicle up with fuel, so I watched the IAM cycling bus trying to get out of the car park, along the very narrow road and out on to the main dual carriage way. That was hysterical! It got stuck again halfway out into the main road and it took some Gendarmes with guns to sort out the chaos that caused. Not sure why it was always IAM, but they also had to move the Mechanics Truck within the car park to reach some plug-in point or other and that went a bit chaotic as well.

I met some lovely people in the hotel. One couple from Holland were watching their 30th consecutive Tour. They were fascinating. They also watched the Classics, or 1-day races so were massive Cycling fans. They were also very fit and healthy as they cycled a lot and had done for years.

I met a Belgian dad and his two teenage daughters who lived in Andorra. He had taken his daughters to the top of Arcalis the day before to watch the race and they had not wanted to go at all. However, he said that at the end they did not want to come back down they had enjoyed it so much! They were going to watch the start of stage 10 as well now.

I got talking to the Ford guy out in the car park again. His job was to keep the fleet of Ford cars running smoothly and efficiently, especially the Mustang which was not totally suited for the terrain. He took the picture of me sitting in the driving seat of the Mustang but refused to let me drive it! Shame. Everyone in the Team Sky camp was so approachable and would talk to anyone. The IAM and Fortuneo teams were approachable too, but my French is dreadful and my Spanish non-existent.

By about 11 all the riders had gone so I decided to go back to the underground hotel spa again as it was brilliant. I was the only one in there same as the day before. From the Jacuzzi beds, I could see into the Gym where the skinniest teenager I have ever seen was working out. As I had noticed him eat solidly for about 40 minutes at breakfast, I deduced that he must work out a lot! Budding cyclist I assume as he was with the IAM cycling group.

Once all the riders had returned from their rides, and had lunch in the various trucks or dining rooms, they all go up to their rooms to put their feet up. Literally according to Rod. Some of the Team Sky staff then went out for their own rides, the Director Sportifs, Sir Dave Brailsford, a few others. They were going to get seriously wet. One of the DS's said he was not wet at all when he got back as he dripped all over the floor. Meantime, the rest day ride bikes needed to be cleaned again, and then packed away. There always seemed to be someone's bike that needed washing or changing in some way. And there were still many fans milling around the car park area just watching everything that is going on.

I love people watching, its such fun.

Later that afternoon, the riders came back down again to meet family and friends in the lounge area. I set up again at my table with another coffee just to watch everything. I could have gone over to speak to any of them, but I decided not to as they had enough of that without me adding to it. I did speak to Rod again though. And the Ford guy who shared my table and joined me for a coffee. He let me see the Tour de France official Handbook. It has all the info in it that the teams need to get around France. It has detailed descriptions of the race route but also details exactly what route all the infrastructure must take including the caravan. And what time everyone must leave, and in what order. All the buses must be at the start tomorrow by 9.30 which is early, and it looks like the trucks, vans and non-race vehicles must take a massive detour through Spain to get to Carcassonne for the start of stage 11. That looked like it would take about 4 hours as it was on good roads but miles further.

The guide also has lists of every hotel that each team will stay in. It is a fascinating guide but only available to the teams themselves, not the public. Not to worry, you can find anything out online if you ask the right questions. What was useful for me though was to know that unless I wanted to go miles out of my way through Spain, I would be best to have lunch somewhere early after the race left on the way out of Andorra and wait for the race to move on before going through the tunnel and down the same road out of Andorra as I had used to come in.

I had a fabulous day, and I got some reasonable pictures as well. The ones of the riders in the hotel all came out ok and the ones from the car park I think show just what I mean by the volume of vehicles needed for just nine riders. The picture looking into the Team Sky Mechanics Truck is one of my favourites as there is so much stuff in it, yet it is cleaner and tidier than my house ever gets!

Later that evening I went out for dinner and to have a look at where the next day's start would be. I wanted to find the best place to stand to see what I wanted to see. The Ford guy came with me as it was his first time on any bike race, and he had not been able to see anything except the team hotels. I really enjoyed talking to him as he knew nothing about the bike race before he was given the opportunity to represent Ford at this year's Tour. He was able to fill me in on much of the logistics of moving the team from hotel to hotel and what his role was within the team set up.

The usual barriers were already up and there was a car park that had been set aside for the team buses with the sign on podium on the opposite side of the road. The best place to stand and watch was going to be a narrow section of barriers along which the riders would go to get to the podium. It was gone 10 by the time I got back to the hotel, but Andorra was still in full swing. I had another long drive the next day though so needed sleep.

I was up early again the next day. Far too much excitement. I headed down to breakfast about 8 with the intention of spending as long as I could there. Loads of the team's staff were also at breakfast and I spoke to several of the people I had accosted the day before. I also saw the skinny teenager eating his way through vast quantities of food again. No idea where he put it all.

I had already agreed with the hotel that I could leave my car in their underground carpark until after the race had left but I did need to vacate my room by 10. I loaded my car and then headed to the pinch point I had identified the day before. I could have sat in the hotel lobby again and watched everyone leave for the race, but I decided to go to the race start instead. The rest day had already exceeded my expectations by a country mile.

Rest day in Albi, 2019.

The stage finish before the rest day and the stage start after the rest day in Albi were on the same road! I would arrive the day before stage finish, so I had plenty of time to look around and find a good place to watch the expected sprint finish. These are not my favourite things to watch but I hoped to find somewhere between 1000 and 500 metres to go to watch from as that is usually a good view.

I arrived in Albi about 6 pm on Bastille day. The place I had booked for the next 3 nights was difficult to find though. I found the right road but could not figure out which was the right property as it was in the middle of a long line of what looked like small bungalows, but which was not. I eventually spotted a small note on a gate that had my name on it. It directed me through the gate and round to the back of the properties where the hostess met me. The property consists of three large split level houses which all belong to members of the same family, and they had removed all the fencing between the houses to make one large garden with a swimming pool. I am staying in a separate little house along one side of the garden towards the river. I have a lounge diner, fully fitted kitchen and the shower room on the ground floor with the bedroom upstairs. There is also my own patio with sun lounger looking straight up at the Cathedral. It was beautiful!

The garden is on one high bank of the River Tarn and on the opposite bank to the massive Albi Cathedral which is stunning. I have never seen a more beautiful or unique building. It's built of red bricks and when the setting sun hit it the whole building lit up and shone. Amazing.

As its Bastille day, the family were having a party in the garden with food, drink, a live band and about sixty guests! They insisted I joined them! There was a Dutch girl there who spoke excellent English and two girls from Newcastle who turned up with their French Friend! Another guy was from the US. Each family had brought food and drink with them which was laid out on several trestle tables set up in the middle of the garden. So much choice! Flans, Quiches, Soups, hot pies, cakes, pastries, so much food! And different wines, beers, or soft drinks. It was such fun.

At about 11 pm we all gathered at the end of the Garden to watch a spectacular fireworks and laser light display centred over the River and the Cathedral. That went on for 45 minutes. It was very loud as well but with the cathedral as the backdrop and the reflection in the river it was beautiful. Afterwards I made my excuses and headed off to bed. No idea what time the party finished as I just passed out. I slept through till 8 the next morning which is unusual for me. Must have been the food, and the wine!

The hosts had stocked the fridge up with butter, honey, milk, jams, cooked meats, cheese, and other food stuffs ready for breakfast. They then left a basket of fresh bread, croissants, pain au chocolate, and some cakes in a covered basket on the kitchen windowsill. I ate breakfast in the dining area looking up at the Cathedral. It was idyllic. They also had a Senseo coffee maker, so it was perfect.

I had a lazy breakfast, and then spent some time just mooching about before setting off to look around Albi and to find out what was going to be where for the stage finish. It is a sprint finish again so standard layout with the finish going over the Tarn river on a fabulous bridge and then quite steeply up to the finish line along a huge 4 lane road through the centre of the town. The usual Tour infrastructure was already up in the centre of Albi. The hospitality houses alongside the finish line. The zone Technique was also right at the finish line today in a huge carpark off to one side. There was a massive area set aside for the Fan Zone today as well which had free Senseo coffee for the fans. Bonus. Everything was set up all round the finish area, so it was all much easier to get to than normal.

I then wandered off to have a bit of a look round this beautiful city. I did speak to lots of people on my wander. A family from Sussex who wanted to know what to expect as it was their first time at the race. An American, some Aussies, and a lovely French lady.

I went back to the bridge across the river and took a few pictures of the River. There is a second road bridge across the river, and it is stunning! The river is quite spectacular. I then walked into the old town. What a beautiful place. Small side streets with old houses built of red bricks and wooden beams. All the streets are cobbled, and some have cafés, restaurants, and tables all over the roads which are car free. All the streets lead uphill towards the magnificent Red Brick Cathedral. In front of and to one side of the Cathedral there is a large stone paved square.

I went into the Cathedral, and it was stunning. I have tried to think of another word here, but none are strong enough to covey just what it is like! It is tiled inside, and every inch is a riot of colour. It is all small patterns, or a biblical scene, and gilded and embossed. It looks incredible and it's huge. I loved it. I could not use a flash inside, and I have no idea how to switch it off so I could not take any pictures, but you can see it on the internet anyway. I have been to some lovely places during the past 5 years at the tour. Albi has now moved to the top of my list of beautiful places.

I had until 5 ish for the race to arrive so I decided to buy something for lunch and take it back to the house to eat in their lovely garden. I also decided to get a bit of washing done as I am running out of clothes. It is hot here now and the clothes all dried in seconds outside. I also needed another Nana nap. I have learnt to rest at every opportunity, so I do not run out of energy.

I went back out towards the 400 metres to go point as that looked a good place to watch from. Met up with Emma there on a raised path looking down on to the race route. It was a good place to watch the Caravan come past. There was a guy from America there watching his first tour. He was astonished by the Caravan as most people are when they see it for the first time. However, we were too far back to get a good view of the actual race coming past. It was likely to be a sprint finish, so these are best watched from ground level.

We walked down from the raised path and to a point on the bridge across the river. There were few people there, so we had a great view as the race came past. The race was in pieces due the mad way the last 50 kilometres was raced. It was an awesome sight seeing the first bunch come in with the sprinters going full speed with the GC guys hanging on behind them. Then the GC guys who had lost time came past. Then the stragglers. Took some time before the Gruppetto arrived.

Once the race had passed and everything was over it was about 6.30. Emma wanted to try and get to the buses but that would have been impossible due to the crowds. They were parked about 500 metres past the finish line so over 1kilometre away. By the time we had pushed through the crowds, the buses would all have left!

Next option was to climb back up towards the Cathedral and find some dinner. We walked all the way around the square by the Cathedral and eventually settled on a small place with nice seating areas and a good looking menu. The food was amazing! I again took pictures of it. I also had a couple of glasses of Beer as it was very hot, and I was not driving again for 2 days.

Just to reiterate, Albi is lovely! I would recommend anyone to come here for a few days. It the birthplace of Toulouse-Lautrec and has a huge museum to him which I will checkout tomorrow.

Today is the rest day and I felt lazy. It was so hot, low 30's all day. I had a wander round the race route from yesterday and it was all GONE, even the painted logos on the road have gone. The Zone Technique had all gone and been replaced by tomorrows Hospitality Village. The Fan zone had been moved en masse to a new plaza. All over night! Amazing.

I found the place where three of the teams were staying right by where yesterday's finish gantry had been. The road was closed so their vehicles were all over the road outside two different hotels. UAE team, Katusha and Team Sunweb. Lots of bike fettling, vehicle washing, so much activity to watch. I wandered up to loads of people for a chat. Everyone was so friendly even if there was a bit of a language barrier! My French is improving but still basic, my Spanish and Italian are non-existent, but everyone speaks bike, so it is fun really.

Next, I headed back up towards the Cathedral again so I could have a look at all the old buildings spreading out from there. The Toulouse Lautrec museum to one side of the Cathedral was undergoing renovations so I wandered round their beautiful formal gardens instead. The museum looks to have been built in an old ecclesiastical building or a castle. Difficult to tell as its huge and a mixture of round turrets and thick walls all built of bricks.

The other side of the Cathedral is more a mixture of cloisters and monastic style buildings with narrow alleys and overhanging houses. I was just standing next to a small opening in a wall that looked like a small doorway to someone's house, when a lady came over and invited me to follow her through the door. We went through a slightly bendy tunnel and then out into the most amazing space! Two side were cloisters, all arched over walkways. The other two sides were other buildings outer walls. In the middle was an amazing courtyard garden. Beautifully kept with an array of so many colourful flowers. It was cool and idyllic in there. I then followed a separate entrance through more old buildings and another courtyard until I came back out by the cathedral again. Just wow!

Back at the Cathedral square again and they were setting up something for the evening so I decided to return to the lovely Chambre d'hôtel with some lunch and just laze about under the shade of some trees in the garden all afternoon so I could come back later that evening and see what was happening. I walked back on a path high above the river which ran all the way to the bridge the race had gone over. It was so beautiful. Have I mentioned that Albi is beautiful? I have never been anywhere like this before, and I cannot wait to go back one day.

Just over the bridge I found the Orica Bike exchange team, almost next door to where I was staying! I had to stop and see who about which was no-one! It was mid-afternoon and extremely hot, so I let them off.

In the evening, I went to the Cathedral square again and it was also transformed. They were having a proper local festival there. There was a local group of musicians playing local instruments. They were surprisingly good. Lots of people were dancing in front of them doing reels, jigs, polkas, bit like a Ceilidh. All around the outside of the square were local food stalls - Cheeses, Duck, Sausages, a vegetarian stall, fruit, all sorts of stuff. There was also a stall selling Japanese food and a Spanish one with Paella. Local beer as well. There were thousands of people there. They had set out rows and rows of trestle tables for people to sit and eat at once they had purchased their food. The whole place was rammed. There were quite a few members of various teams' staff there enjoying their rest day.

I sat at one of the tables just enjoying the atmosphere and watching the funny dancing. I picked up some local sausage and potatoes from a stall and some tasty cheeses to take back to eat at the house. It was a lovely day and Albi is worth a visit by anyone.

Rest day in Le Puy en Velay, 2017.

I had arrived in Le Puy the day before the finish of stage 14 before the rest day, so I could watch the downhill (see downhill chapter) and would stay until after the roll out of the next stage the day after the rest day. Again, the finish of one stage was the start of the next which is perfect.

The rest day was another sweltering day with not a cloud in the sky, so brolly was at the ready! I felt a bit lazy that day, so I had a bit of a lie in until 7.30 which is late for me! I spent the breakfast chatting to the landlady in our mixture of English and French. She is just lovely. It was the same breakfast as the day before but this time there was a whole bunch of grapes!

My plan for the day was to go to the team hotels I had seen the day before furthest up the hill and then walk back down to the others. As it was so hot and the climb up to the hotel where team Sky were staying was very steep (I rode past it on the way up and on the way down and it was right on top of the 8% section) I decided that I would walk instead. I still melted but it was better than riding! There was a reasonable crowd of fans at the Sky Hotel again but there were hundreds of Media people. When Chris Froome poked his nose out of the hotel to walk to the place he was going to do all the interviews, the scrum that rolled around him was just ridiculous. Anyway, he still came over to the waiting fans and signed everything they had again. He has the patience of a saint!

Just outside the entrance to the hotel and its car park there was a 3 ft high wall which was exactly right for me to sit on and rest as I was totally melting by then in the heat. I sat there just watching what was going on from under my umbrella. (That is the best piece of kit I had with me, and it was a total life saver! People laughed at first, but they were jealous once they melted, and I stayed reasonably ok.) It was quite fascinating. And a bit surreal. There were loads of photographers milling around and to watch them with massive lenses right up close to the bikes taking pictures from about 3 inches away of a bike brake or a piece of cable. Just nuts! And really funny. Also, to watch the TV guys with massive cameras on their shoulders running around and around Froome as he walked along was so funny too.

Rod came over for a nice long chat today. He commented that he had seen me popping up all over the place the last few days. He was really interested to know what I had seen and done. He said he does not get to see any of the actual race himself as he is always just in front of it. He was thinking that one day when he no longer does the Tour of getting a camper van with his wife and kids and seeing what all the fuss is about. We chatted for about 10 minutes today.

I was able to watch as the Katusha Team rode past in formation up the still steep hill. They were just out for a rest day ride so were nowhere near full gas, but they were still moving fast. I managed to get a halfway decent picture of them from my vantage point on the wall which was nice.

After the Sky riders had set off for their rest day ride, I walked back towards the town. I spotted a few more team hotels and stopped at each one for a mooch around and a chat with anyone who stood still long enough. I love doing that. People make the tour for me.

In the town, I decided to do the full tourist bit here and see what was in Le Puy en Velay and it did not disappoint. I headed towards the cathedral on the top of the hill / volcanic plug in the centre of the town. It is a beautiful building with just the most idyllic surroundings of small streets that are barred to cars. From there you can see across to a second volcanic plug pointing straight up in the air. There is a second large church built on the top of this straight plug of rock several hundred feet high and far too much effort to climb up and see in that heat, but it looked like it might be worth the effort if I had had more time. There is a giant red statue the other side of the town on a similar rock plug. Apparently, the statue is made from melted down cannons from the Crimean war. There are then loads of small streets leading down from the Cathedral in all directions, and most of which are made of flint which makes walking tricky. The place was buzzing.

I stopped at a small cafe near the Cathedral for lunch. I had just ordered mine when a lady turned up asking if anyone spoke English. Naturally, I piped up! She wanted to know if she should just sit down and did they come out to see her. She was American and on her own for the first time, ever. Her son who she was travelling with had gone off elsewhere that day. I invited her to come and sit with me as I was also on my own. Her name was Trish, and she was 52. It is her first visit to Europe, and she spoke no French whatsoever. I ordered her food for her, and we had an enjoyable time just sat under an umbrella in a lovely old town on top of a hill by a Cathedral. We talked for ages. She would love to do what I am doing. She is an avid fan of the Tour and watches every year in the US. Her trip was spur of the moment and the idea of her son who was going around the world for 2 months and suggested this would be her best chance to get to the Tour for real. Everyone I meet has a story to tell. We agreed to meet up again later that evening for dinner which was the only plan with another person I made all that holiday.

After lunch, as I walked back to the Chambre d'Hotes, I went through the old marketplace. That had an amazing trio of singers singing old Jazz songs. They were so good. And as it was a market day, the area was also full of pens with Goats, Horses, Chickens, and Sheep! All mixed in with tables from cafes and bars. Simply weird. So French. The whole place was relaxed but a hive of activity. And so pretty. If you ever want to go somewhere that is typically French, incredibly beautiful, remarkably interesting, and incredibly old, then this is the place you should go. I just loved it. Maybe I should charge the French Tourist Board commission. But it really is idyllic.

I went along to the other teams Hotels to see what was happening there but by then all the riders should have been resting in their rooms. It was also a bit difficult to get into most of their hotels this time which was a shame. I wanted to try and sit in a foyer or something and just watch what was going on, but the Hotels were all just too small to allow for that. The car parks with the team's vehicles and mechanics in were still busy with bike fettling and stuff though which I could watch. Movistar had their giant Mechanics truck just parked on the side of a main road!

Later that evening I met up with Trish and her son Cody in a restaurant that had been recommended to them by the owners of where they were staying. That is where I found out that Puy Lentils come from Le Puy en Velay! Who Knew?! Naturally, I had to have some just to try them. They were delicious and simply served with a piece of steamed Salmon.

After dinner, I set off to see what was happening in the town as it was absolutely buzzing. Every corner seemed to have a live band on it. All sorts of music including a group doing Elvis covers. There was also a group including a drummer, set up on trailers and being pulled round town behind bikes. The Jazz trio were still there, and I listened to them for some time, they were so good. Everywhere was set up for just sitting outside and watching something going on. I had a wonderful time listening to live music, people watching. My favourite pastime.

At around 10 pm the whole town lights up. The main monuments have a sort of laser light show done on them every night in the summer. It was excellent, but my phone battery was flat, so I got no pictures. I loved Le Puy en Velay and if I ever get the chance I will go back.

Back at the Hotel, I wrote Rod a letter to thank him for everything he had done for me this tour. I was able to give it to him at the start the next day. I had added my e-mail address, and I was stunned to get an e-mail from him a few days later just to make sure I had got home ok. He is the nicest, kindest man in the world!

Hints and tips.

Finding teams hotels is not that hard. Just look online for large hotels in the area that look to have some parking and you will probably find a team there. You can also look at social media as often someone will give the game away!

Visiting team hotels is interesting on many levels, not least finding out just how many people and vehicles it takes to get 8 riders round the Tour de France!

The rest day is also a good opportunity to discover either the area or the town if you can. The race route takes you to unusual places all round France so make the most of it!

Downhills

What goes up must come down! Watching them go up hill is obviously impressive, but a downhill is something else. The speed the riders reach is unbelievable. And I highly recommend any one of a strong constitution to watch one.

Sunday, 16th July 2017. Le Puy en Velay.

I had by then been travelling round France on my own for 14 days and it was beginning to catch up with me. I had cycled up three Category 1 climbs so far this tour, so I felt justified in being a bit tired. However, I was staying in the same place for three nights as it would be the rest day here this year, which would allow me time to recover a bit.

I had the usual bready breakfast, but there were grapes and a nice yogurt as well this time. The coffee was again terrible and served in a large bowl, but it was better than the tea! I love staying in these Chambre d'Hotes. Real French houses with real French people instead of Hotel chains staffed by cloned employees, although I do like the hotels as well.

The race was due to arrive at about 5 pm on the section I had identified as my target today. I was going to cycle to the top of the final climb from the wrong side and then watch the race on the final run down to the finish line in the centre of Le Puy en Velay. No rush today at all, fortunately. I had time to wander through the town looking at all the activities going on around the finish line before cycling out to the hills.

All the usual miles of barriers were already up and seemed to be going all the way round the outside of the whole town. They covered at least the last 2 kilometres of the race. The Podium was also already up, the finish gantry and the VIP stands were still being unfolded. The finish line advertising was still being drawn on the ground under the gantry. They were using giant stencils and a spray paint gun to put the Skoda markings and logos around the actual finish line. Quite interesting to watch that as again, it is just not something you think about when you just watch the finish on the TV. I could also see them aligning the camera used to decide who wins in a photo finish.

The Media village was just behind the finish line today. That is unusual as it needs such a big car park or open space to fit it all in. I watched the France TV2 "house" being unfolded. It is quite something to see. When fully extended it is three stories high, with bi-fold doors opening onto a patio. It is huge. And they have a separate 'house' that has an open roof top area with large canopies over it where they have their studio set up for interviews and the post-race shows. They also have a huge outdoor dining area set up under canopies with tables covered in white linen tablecloths. For 100's of people.

Other TV crews have similar set ups but France TV2 is the biggest.

There were miles and miles of cables going in every direction between the houses and the power supplies. No idea where they get all the power they need from. Not sure a socket would do! I assume they all have generators, but these are often difficult to spot.

I returned to the Chambre d'Hotes to get into my cycling kit and pack ready to cycle the 13.6 kilometres to the summit at Saint Vidal, a Category 4 climb from the race direction but longer and less steep from the direction I was going. The landlady was there as I was about to leave and had made me up a packed lunch! That was so kind of her. She wrapped each item separately in foil to keep fresh as well. There was also a huge tomato in a Tupperware pot, but I just could not fit that into my backpack. Left it in my car and ate it another day.

I set off on my bike towards the start as I needed to attempt to reverse follow the Tour route out of town. It was not as easy as it sounds as the roads had all been closed alongside the actual race route all with barriers all over them so picking the right barriers to follow is tricky. And the green arrows (tour signs denoting the route that ASO attach to various lamp posts and road signs all along the race route each day) all pointed the wrong way! I had to ask a Gendarme for directions in the middle of the town as I was already lost.

I eventually headed out of town on the right road, and it went sharply up hill, over 10 %, which reduced me to walking very quickly. I managed a mixture of walking and riding for the first 4 kilometres then it levelled off a bit and was a steady 5 - 6 % the rest of the way. I was at the top of the climb by 1.30 pm and that was including all the stopping and chatting I did. I felt much easier riding up the climb that day than I had done in the Pyrenees, so I knew I was getting fitter just over these few days. And of course, it was not the Pyrenees which are considerably steeper!

I met a couple from Flanders who were keen cyclists but only on the flat. I also bumped into to two girls from York! They had driven along a side road to get as close to the top as they could much earlier in the day, then parked and walked about 5 kilometres to the top. There were hundreds of people cycling in the same direction as me and even more coming up the other side of the col. There was the usual collection of stalls, and barriers and other temporary buildings around the summit. It is amazing just how much equipment, stalls, banners, port-a-loos, barriers, etc, is carted round France and deposited on top of mountains, at intermediate sprints, at feed stations, and numerous points all over the stages each day. Someone had also built this sort of aerial roundabout from which they had hung two bicycles on which they were riding! Looked a bit dicey to me. And it was very wobbly!

I took some pictures of the summit then cycled back down to just past the 10 kilometres to go banner. I had spotted this place on the way up and it looked ideal. A nice wide grass verge, recently cut with the cuttings left to dry out in the sun, some trees for shade and an unobstructed view across a wide road in the middle of a long straight downhill section. Just what I had hoped for.

I set up camp under the shade of a screen of tall trees on the freshly cut dry grass. It was nice and soft to lie on. I put my brolly up, blew up another IBIS cushion (these are thrown from the Caravan each day and I collected as many as I could as they were so useful), and settled down to do some crossword puzzles from my book. Fortunately, I was covered in Sun Cream as I promptly fell fast asleep! By the time I woke up, the sun had moved, and I was not in the shade anymore. My Brolly had protected most of me though. I snore dreadfully so I hope I did not disturb the neighbours on the hillside too much.

My lunch was lovely. Half a Baguette with a thick slice of ham and the other half with a giant wedge of Blue Brie. There was also a pot of Fruit Puree (looked like a yogurt pot) and a large apple. I wish I could have brought the Tomato though as that would have been perfect. I was able to enjoy my meal, sat at the roadside watching everything unfold ready for the race to arrive much later. I also had snacks with me and some of my usual fruit store, so I certainly did not go hungry. I had taken two bottles of water and two bottles of diluted Orange Juice with me which was enough for that day even though it was extremely hot.

By the time I woke up, I was no longer alone on the side of the road. A few hundred people had stationed themselves on both sides of the road but there was plenty of room for everyone here. I stayed by myself today. It was my choice as I could easily have spoken to anyone but sometimes, I just like to be by myself and relax in my own way. That, I think, is the beauty of doing this trip by myself. I can do whatever I feel like at the time and not have to worry about changing any plans. And it is way better than trying to go on a package holiday on your own! Apart from having to pay extra I always got 'adopted' by some family or other who just cannot accept that I can be happy just being by myself. I am sure anyone who has ever tried this knows just what I am talking about here.

The caravan came through and I got loads more rubbish even though I was hiding under my brolly again. I did manage to get two cartons of orange juice and about five packets of Haribo's so not all bad. I also managed to replenish my stock of Ibis cushions. It was incredibly hot out there today and the caravan people were looking a bit tired and less up for anything. Not so annoyingly happy. Still, it was the rest day tomorrow and I guess that would refresh their batteries.

Finally, the race came through and I got a halfway decent video this time. Not brilliant of course but I can hear the noise of the wheels and see how fast they are going on the video. It is such a varied sensory experience when the riders go past – power, speed, noise, colour, so many different aspects all missed by the TV coverage. The breakaway was a long way in front of the peloton at this point and it is just astonishing how fast they are going. Bauke Mollema was in the lead all on his own with about ten guys trying desperately to catch him up. The slope was not particularly steep here, but the road was very wide and straight, so they were going full tilt. When the peloton came past that had fractured into multiple groups which all came hurtling past over the next 30 minutes or so. The sprinters and bigger guys at the back of the race were amazing at going fast downhill. It may be because they go slower up the hills first and need to catch back up, or that they are generally heavier, but they just seem to float effortlessly downhill so fast.

Once I had packed up all the rubbish from the caravan into my backpack, I then had to carry it all back down the mountain. I have bags of the stuff in my car now! I rode down as fast as I dared but I was going so much slower than the riders!

—⟐⟐⟐—

Thursday, 20th July 2022. Col d'Aspin.

The first mountain I climbed at the tour was the Col d'Aspin. I have such happy memories from my first visit in 2015. It will be different this time though as I am going to the other side of the Col to watch the race come downhill instead.

Driving around the Pyrenees can be a bit complicated. There are so many huge mountains all right next to each other with long winding river valleys in between that the route can wriggle around a bit. The Col d'Aspin starts near Arreau. Over the top and at the foot of the downhill, it is only about 7 kilometres to the foot of the Tourmalet. If you go left at the foot of the Col d'Aspin then you are also at the foot of the Hourquette d'Anzican. Over that one and you are near the Val Lauron and the Pla d'Adet mountains. Working out where to go and what to see on this stage took ages. In the end, as I fancied watching a downhill, and I knew how to get there from just south of Lourdes where I was staying, the Col d'Aspin was my eventual choice. I had a summit finish to ride up the next day too so that was also a factor.

The plan was to drive to St Marie de Campan, which is where the road forks with the Tourmalet going right and the Col d'Aspin going left. I would then drive as far as I could, turn round so I was pointing the right way, and leave the car under a tree if I could find one. Did not go to plan as far too many people had the same idea. However, I did manage it eventually and had just 5 kilometres to cycle to the foot of the col.

I decided to cycle up a bit of the Col d'Aspin just because I had loads of time today. The area here is so pretty, with lots of trees and forests. I was in no hurry, so I stopped and chatted with quite a few people who had set up camp on the way up. It also gave me an opportunity to find a good place to watch from. That turned out to be all the way back towards the foot of the climb. From there I could watch them come out of the trees, down a long, straight, wide open section of road, round a corner at the bottom, then along to the junction, left along a flat part and then hit the bottom of the next climb. I had my binoculars with me, so I had an astonishing view.

I set up my camp on the wide grassy area with my Brolly up as usual. Lunch, liquids, puzzle book, people to talk to if I wanted to, perfect.

On the Tour de France, there are 5 VIP helicopters that ferry people along the race route each day. I see them everywhere. I even managed to get a ride in one once (see "How lucky am I days")! They need to find large flat open spaces to land during the race, and they picked my grassy area to land on today. Quite a remarkable sight five large helicopters landing just below you in formation.

Just after they landed, I spotted some smoke coming from near the corner where the race turned left. A building was on fire! Quite a large building, with a thatch roof. It had really caught hold and the whole building was engulfed. I could see flames in among the heavy smoke. After about 20 minutes of burning, a fire engine drove towards it from d'Anzican along the race route the wrong way, just as the first riders were coming off the d'Aspin! It was touch and go as to who would get to the corner first. The fire engine just managed to get out of the way before the riders arrived. That bit was not on the TV coverage. Can only happen at the tour.

I watched the breakaway riders zoom down the mountains, ride fast to the corner, then get back up to speed before the foot of the next mountain. It was awesome. The GC guys came passed next going so fast. Everyone else came passed in small bunches for about the next 20 minutes. It was amazing. They all made it look so easy which it certainly is not! Such a great place to watch from.

On the cycle back to the car, I went passed the building that caught fire. There was nothing left but a pile of ash! Burnt to the ground!

I cycled back to the car, drove back to Lourdes, shower then out for dinner in a place I had checked out the day before. They had Paella! And it was huge! Delicious.

Hints and tips.

Try and find a long, straight section of road to watch a downhill as they come past so fast you need time to see them!

Do not get too close to the edge of the road. That is too scary!

I doesn't matter if the peloton is all together or split to pieces when they come past, it is still spectacular.

Hilly Stages

These take many forms, and each provides many differences as to what you can expect see. Mid points, short sharp stage ends, gently rolling all day with sprint finishes. Anything is possible on these days.

Thursday, 11th July 2018. Mûr-de-Bretagne.

I am staying in my own little bungalow for the next 3 nights. It is just off the stage 6 race route in a small village that does not seem to have any facilities at all. I had already checked out the food opportunities before I left home so I made use of the large supermarket at the previous stop to stock up on food to cook that first evening. My plan was to get to the Bungalow 2 days before the race arrived on the Tuesday, as I could get to stage 5's start from there easily. I try and stay as many days as possible in one place, so I am not moving to a new place every day. It is much less tiring that way. Also, as the race was going to go up the Mur twice, it was worth the extra stay!

The drive to the Mur was easy but then it got a bit complicated as I tried to get to the bungalow itself. The race arrives here the evening of 11th to ride up the very steep Mur (hill) and already they had closed the road. I had to go miles round the back roads to get here as I am staying right at the end of the stage just past the finish line. The bungalow is fabulous. I have the whole house and garden to myself. It is nice with a fully fitted kitchen, shower room, laundry room and lounge diner downstairs and a bedroom covering the whole footprint of the bungalow up a spiral staircase on a mezzanine. It is all old stone walls and beams everywhere. They also had a washing machine and a drying line in the garden! Very handy.

I went out for a walk once I had settled in just to see what was what and where. In a field on the edge of the village there is an entire Campervan village again. At least 50 of them with others scattered wherever they can get on any grass verge or lay-by etc. Unlike me though, they were all stuck there and could not just drive off to see the start the next day. Quite a few parties going on with them though, so I guess they all enjoyed doing this. I have thought a few times about hiring a campervan to follow the tour but, for me, it is too limiting unless you can cycle more than 100 kilometres, which I cannot.

The village I was in was quaint. It was small with one shop that doubled as a bar. The shop only opened early morning for a few hours and then again around 5 ish till 7. If you wanted to buy any bread, you had to order it the day before. There were some large houses in the centre and a huge church. It was incredibly quiet there, but I expected things to change in 2 days' time when the tour invaded it!

After seeing the start of stage 5, I drove back to the bungalow easily as I knew about the road closures. However, I was looking for somewhere to buy some more water and a few supplies but it's Wednesday and France seems to shut again in the afternoon. I had to wait for the small shop to re-open to get some. It did have water but not much else. Should have bought stuff in the start town, but I forgot France closes so early on a Wednesday.

I went out this evening to see what the end of the Stage 6 looks like. My bungalow, I thought, was about 100 meters from the finish line down a side street. I walked towards the race route and to what I thought would be the stage finish point. It wasn't! It was the bonus sprint point! The actual stage finish was down a steep hill and then up over the top of another one. Good job I had a bike with me. That was about 4 kilometres in total. That whole race route in the area will be closed from Midnight tonight and the actual finish straight has been closed for at least 2 days already.

The tour will arrive overnight tonight and be all set up by the time I get up tomorrow. I took some pictures of the empty road at around 5 pm today so I can capture the difference tomorrow. Usually, the whole 3 kilometres of the Mur is barriered off on both sides of the road. That is a lot of barriers to put up overnight. Plus the Finish Gantry, the Presentation Podium, and somewhere an entire media village will have to be accommodated. The lorries that transport everything around must also be put somewhere. Will be interesting to see how they do this, but the tour has finished here many times before, so it is all well planned. I took before and after photos just to be able to compere the overnight changes.

I had a relaxing evening in my own little bungalow. I cooked myself a nice tea with some cold beers and just sat out in the garden under the stars. Lovely.

Next morning, it was still hot here and standing in the sun for 4 hours each day is very tiring. I could not do it without the Brolly. Lots of people got well burnt today. Anyway, it is nice staying in my own little house. I had a lazy morning, bit of a lie in, some eggs for a late breakfast, cup of proper tea, etc. Nice.

I needed to ride the 4 kilometres to the end of the stage today so I packed my backpack with everything I would need, set up my bike and rode towards the stage end at about midday. The downhill was OK, but the following uphill was steep. I managed to ride all bar the last 100 metres though so that was great.

The entire Media village was on one side of the top of the Mur, including the 50ft crane with the satellite dishes on top. It covered a few acres with multiple lorries that open out into small houses. The podium was on the same side of the road but nearer to the race route. The usual booths were opened out for the Commentators as were the 3 hospitality houses. On the opposite side of the road was a large multi-tiered stand for VIP's and parking for shed loads of tour vehicles. There was a clutch of marquees some way off to one side of the route as well as parking for five helicopters.

There was also a group of stalls selling tour memorabilia and local stalls selling mainly food just before I reached the finish line.

It was 4 hours before the race was due and every inch of the side of the road leading from the bottom of the climb to the finish line had been claimed by hordes of fans. For at least 3 kilometres on both sides of the road. I left my bike padlocked to a sapling near where the Helicopters were parked and set off to find a place to watch from. I managed to find these lovely French people and they moved over to let me in around the 150 to go marker just where the gradient lessened off a bit. I had an excellent view down the slope a short way, and up towards the finish line. The road curved round to the left so I could not actually see the finish line though.

For the next 4 hours the crowds were entertained by a host of different sponsors singing, dancing and being really cheerful. They gave out so much free stuff it was insane. T shirts from Skoda (green Jersey) and Carrefour (polka dot Jersey), lots of caps in Yellow, Polka dot, Krys blue ones (young riders jersey), loads of bottles of water from Vittel (and I do mean loads!). There was someone in a full chicken costume and another in a Lizard costume walking up and down Another person was dressed as a washing machine. Seen him at all the Tours I have been on. The Cochonou guy was cycling his barrow up and down the finish area too, giving out loads of Salami on small slices of toasted bread. The chicken, Lizard, and a few others had a race. Very funny. This all made the time pass quickly.

The Caravan came past again with about 2 hours to go before the race turned up for the first time. It was the usual madness. When the race came past first time, I was waving my Yorkshire flag just in case the TV cameras pointed in my direction. It was an amazing sight this time as the riders were still all together in a bunch and going so fast. No one was off the front at that point.

The race came back around 20 minutes later with Dan Martin really giving it everything just ahead of the rest of the field. He was too close to the barrier I was leaning over to get the picture right. Never mind, it was still awesome. I watched as all the rest came past slow enough to actually see this time. Not like the sprint finishes which are just too fast. However, they were still going at a considerable speed.

Things then got a bit complicated. The Buses were all parked off to one side at the foot of the Mur, so the riders had to ride down the Mur as well, so I got some pictures of them going in both directions at once! No idea where to look to see what. The ones still coming up were not worried about the time cut today so were enjoying the ride up. They were waving to the crowds and relaxing all the way up.

I also spotted Lawson Craddock again. He is still covered in bandages from the injuries he sustained on the first few kilometres of the very first stage. He is the 'Lantern Rouge' or last man on the race. He has a broken shoulder blade so is in dreadful pain. He comes from New Orleans and has been tweeting out that he will donate $100 for every stage he completes to rebuilding their Velodrome that was destroyed in the Hurricane and asking others to match his funds. He has so far raised thousands of Dollars. Lance Armstrong and Chris Froome both re-tweeted his initial Tweet, so the coverage went up rapidly. And he is still going!

I then had to get out of the scrum, retrieve my bike and cycle down then up back to my house. Got back about 6.30 ish. I again rode all the downhill and about half the uphill as it was steep. I cooked myself some tea then went out into the town to see what was going on as I could hear some live music from the garden. I found it in the centre of the town, but it was not worth staying for, so I came back. I packed my bike away in the car, loaded up my suitcase and relaxed as I had an exceedingly long day ahead of me the next day.

Saturday 16th July 2022. Mende.

I had the entire morning to relax before walking up to the finish line about 4 kilometres from where I am staying. I was only 200 metres from the race route. The finish is on the aerodrome runway at the top of a very steep 4 kilometre hill. In hindsight, I should have taken my bike, but I didn't because it is so steep, I knew I could not ride it at all. The walk back though, was dreadful! Way too hot.

I went to the shop first, to buy some supplies for lunch and dinner as it was just too hot to do anything else. I bought quite a lot of Orange juice as a method of rehydrating as it is easier to drink more water if you add a little orange juice to it. I also bought some bananas as they help replenish all the salts lost through sweat. The apartment I was staying in had a freezer, so I topped up my frozen bidons for the day with orange juice too. The rest went into the fridge for later.

For information, I had G's Gilet! In the first stages of the tour in Denmark, there had been an individual time trial and Geraint Thomas (INEOS) had worn a gilet over his seriously aero and expensive skin suit during his warmup. He then forgot to take it off! He rode the ITT with it still on negating all the aero benefits from his skin suit. He got so much stick for that on social media, it was so funny. He and the INEOS social media guy, George, decided to use this to have some fun of their own.

The plan was to pass the gilet from fan to fan and try and get the gilet all the way round the race route to Paris. I chatted with George about this via messages and produced "Gilet Relay" as a name. George adapted this to "G'lay Relay" which was excellent. The Gilet passed to me from the Beefeaters in Bourg d'Oisans which was the start of the previous stage. I was to pass it on in Mende to the next relay fan.

I was expected to carry the Gilet in my car for an entire day, but it had been worn by so many people in extreme heat, worn by fans sweating up hills, been sprayed by beer and other liquids, and god knows what else, so it was minging! It could almost stand up on its own! Everyone had also signed it to say they were part of the relay. I had some very mild detergent with me, so I washed it. Probably should have worn gloves and a hazmat suit, but it came out quite well without losing any of the signatures.

I set off about 2 pm allowing an easy 90 minutes to walk to the top before the caravan arrived. A lady from Spain had messaged me that morning asking that I stop by them with the Gilet as they wanted to see it. I met them at the 2 kilometre to go banner. The whole family was there, and all kitted out in INEOS kit with several Welsh flags! They were huge fans of Geraint Thomas. I was able to let each of them try it on and take photos and they were so happy. That is the Tour de France in a nutshell right there for me. Their English was a bit limited, and my Spanish is non-existent, but we managed to chat for ages.

A bit further along, there was a gang of road workers with spades and 'Big Bertha' which is a giant road sweeper that goes along the entire tour route, making sure any loose debris is removed, digging up and flattening a section of the road that had been burned by a car on fire! The car had been put out and dragged off. They then had a matter of a few hours to repair the road. There is no way you get to see this sort of thing on the TV. I am not sure they even know it happens.

I carried on up the ridiculously steep hill to the top and across the carpark beside the runway to the 200 metres to go post and set up camp there. I had an excellent view all the way down the runway to the bend at the start of the finish straight (about 500 metres), and then towards the finish gantry 200 metres away. Perfect. And I was there before the Caravan.

There were lots of sponsors wandering up and down giving away their goodies. I was given several cans of drink which turned out to be alcohol free fruit beer and it was horrible! I managed to drink one can but that was it. I only had two bidons of liquid with me as it's too heavy and bulky to carry. (Needed my bike even if I only pushed it).

They were also giving away packets of butter biscuits which were delicious. And some fruit which is always useful. I had attached the Gilet to the 200 metres to go sign just in case anyone spotted it. There were not too many people at the top that day though, probably because of the extreme heat. It was well into the mid 40 degrees centigrade and without shade, the sun physically hurt. My Factor 50 Sunshade / Umbrella was essential.

Emma joined me eventually and we sat down to await the race which we could watch on the big screen on the other side of the course. Such a fast finish after climbing up that hideously steep hill. Michael Matthews won. Brilliant. Everyone else came past in dribs and drabs after the GC contenders led the peloton home several minutes behind the winner.

It was so hot today. Almost melted. Without my Brolly, I would have. How the riders managed I have no idea. After the race, the plan was to walk round to the buses which were parked behind the airport building just beside the finish line. We had to walk round the back of the building to get there which was easier said than done but we did it eventually. Unfortunately, we did not get to see anyone at the buses this time. But we did get to speak to Gary (Israel Premier Tech team). He asked if I was OK, did I have enough water, was I ok in the heat, etc. I was but he gave us a bottle of cold water each which I drank straight away.

Emma unfortunately did not with the expected repercussions later. It was then just a case of walk the 4 kilometres back down the mountain. We both had brollies, but Emma started to lag behind me on the way down. Eventually she put her brolly down too! I did not notice as I was still just walking steadily downwards.

I reached the point where the road I was staying on met the race route and turned to say bye to Emma and she wasn't there. I went back up the road and found her round the next bend fortunately, but she was obviously suffering from heat stroke. She had no idea where she was. I dragged her to the start of my road where she collapsed. I left her with a French Family while I got my car. We managed to tip her into to it, drive 200 metres to my front door and I finally got her indoors and out of the heat.

2 hours later, after several cold towels for her head and copious amounts of orange juice and cold water which I forced her to drink, she started to come round. In the end, I drove her back to her digs as there was no way I could let her wander round Mende on her own. I was supposed to hand over the Gilet to her as well, but I kept it for another day instead. I offered to take her to Carcassonne, so I guess technically, she did have the Gilet. We handed it over together at the finish the next day. Heat Stroke creeps up so easily. You do not feel thirsty and if you do not force liquids into yourself, then you will likely find yourself in difficulties in the heat of the south of France!

George had told Geraint that I had washed the Gilet and Geraint tweeted about it and copied me in! My Twitter account went nuts!

Sunday, 9th July 2023. Puy de Dome.

This stage was an obvious one to go to when the route came out. The Puy de Dome is a huge volcanic plug that had been used once before in the tour and is easily accessible from Clermont Ferrand which was the host city for the following rest day, with another stage starting one side of the city and finishing the other having gone all round the Volcanic national park. Finally, the stage after that started in the city centre. Three stages and a rest day all accessible from one place is fantastic and exceedingly rare! Because I need to stay in a place that has a space for my car, I had provisionally booked an apartment the previous September, based on rumours of what the route would probably be. It meant I had one in the perfect place once the route finally came out a month later.

The Apartment when I got there was lovely. Incredibly quiet with just one room for the bed, kitchen and sitting area all divided by net screens. No Air con but there was a highly effective fan! The bathroom was off to one side with a laundry next to it. I did have to negotiate an outside spiral staircase to get to a small balcony and the front door, but I managed it. The car park was underground so nice a cool.

Its Sunday today. That means France is mostly shut all day. Fortunately, there was a supermarket 200 metres away that opened for a few hours on a Sunday morning. I bought croissants for my breakfast, a sandwich for my lunch, and a microwavable paella with some salad for my tea. Plus more fruit and orange juice.

My plan for the stage was to cycle the 9 kilometres to the base of the Puy de Dome and then see if I could leave my bike somewhere and walk towards the top. Jamie from the Gilet wearers WhatsApp group is here, and he went out early (9 ish) to cycle up to the finish to check it out. He fed back that it is steep at the start of the climb, which is right outside my apartment, and the final 6 kilometres of the race is totally closed to everyone, cycling or walking. Even the team cars and buses were directed off the race route to a car park at that point. That meant I did not need to cycle as I could walk the 2 or 3 kilometres to where I identified as the next best place to watch from. That also meant I did not need to leave early as the race was not due until 5 ish that afternoon.

It does not matter how detailed your plans are, they still need to be a bit flexible. If you do not take any changes as a negative, and enjoy whatever else you get to experience, then it's still all good being there to watch.

After watching the early part of the race on tv, I left to meet Jamie round the corner from my apartment. We then walked up to a great viewpoint over the surrounding volcanic landscape where we were meeting Ruth and Matt and some of their friends from Wales. I have met so many people over the years that it is nice to have people to meet up with each year.

The walk up was very steep indeed. And the temperature was so hot! Low 40 degrees centigrade with no wind. It was stifling. There was no air at all. I have no idea how the riders coped with riding in this. I was ringing wet after a few minutes of walking. We walked really slowly.

It is a beautiful place though. We came out of the built up area quickly and the Vulcania National Park is stunning. I have always been interested in landscapes and geological features, so this was heaven to me. Where some of the hills had been eroded it was possible to see the hexagonal granite columns that were formed by the volcanic eruptions and everywhere you looked, there were the small, pointy hills of volcanic plugs.

We met a Mountie! In full kit with a Canadian flag! He must have been roasted as he even had the boots on.

We reached Ruth who was so easy to spot as she had fixed several huge Welsh flags to the cliff behind her and had a nice long chat with her and her friends. There were too many people there though and there was a much better place to watch from about 100 metres back down the hill. The road was at least three lanes wide with a shallow bend between two long straight sections of road. On the outside of that bend was a great place to watch from and there were not many people there either.

When the race came past, one of my favourite riders, Mike Woods, chasing three riders that were still in front of him. You could see just how much faster he was going than the others were. He did catch them and won the stage. The GC riders came past next, and they were also racing hard and going even faster than Woods! The rest of the riders were all over the race route, going so much slower. It was an excellent place to watch from and I managed to get some great video and some good pictures.

It was then a short walk back to my apartment, a shower as I was melting, and a bowl of hot soapy water to soak my feet in as they were wrecked! I did get an excellent picture of the Puy de Dome a few days later (see "How lucky am I days!").

Hints and tips.

These days can offer so much. Often there will be a breakaway, so you get two races for the price of one.

These short, sharp finishes are explosive and great to watch. However, there are lots of people squeezed into a shorter area, so it can be crowded.

If you drive, then check out the route closures in advance as they will be extensive.

On some stages, for the better cyclists among you, there is the opportunity to cycle over several climbs if you feel so inclined.

If you decide to go by campervan then be warned. There are hundreds of them at most hilly finishes so you will need to arrive a few days prior to the race.

Most of the interesting points on these stages are miles from anywhere! Public transport would need to be thoroughly checked out before you leave for France.

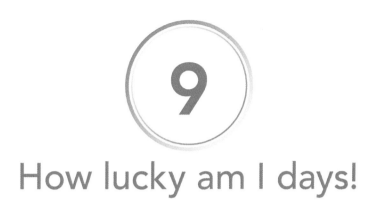

How lucky am I days!

Tuesday, 11th July 2023. Vulcania to Issoire.

I tend to talk to anyone who will stand still long enough, which is how I have met so many lovely people over the years. One of these is John Trevorrow, former three times Australian National Road Cycling Champion. He talks nearly as much as I do so it was inevitable that we would meet eventually. He is such a nice man. He is affiliated but not part of the Jayco Alula team. This year, apart from doing his TV work for SBS, interviewing people at the starts, he was driving one of the Jayco Alula team cars and handing out bidons and bags at various points along the stages.

I had met him several times already this tour and had lots of chats about grandchildren. He has even more than I do.

During the rest day in Clermont Ferrand, John messaged to say I could go in the Jayco Alula team car with him for tomorrow's stage if I wanted to. That stage was going in a big loop all-round the Vulcania national park starting and finishing just outside Clermont Ferrand. He would even pick me up and drop me back at my apartment as that was near the Jayco Hotel, so naturally I said yes please!!!

John and his fellow bidon provider Vaz, picked me up about 9.15 and drove to the start. The road was closed to only tour traffic, but it still took forever to get through. The start was at 13.05 and we parked up just after 10.40. Some of the team buses were still behind us at that point. John and Vas then headed off to do interviews, etc.

I had an access all areas pass for the day which meant I could get into the village depart for the first time this tour. I took some pictures of that and of the free food and drink on offer. It was set up in a wooded area so was pleasantly cool in the shade.

Christian Prudhomme (ASO chief) was on the podium set up in the village, interviewing some VIP's. Someone was wandering round in a black skin suit with bright yellow flashes and a large yellow plastic helmet on. I assume it was supposed to be some sort of superhero, but I had no idea which one.

The stand with the Bio Foods was here with some free samples. The usual Chicken and Chips stall had someone making these excellent kebabs of various sun dried vegetables. So much to see here but I had a deadline today. I had to be back at the car by 12.15 as we were going to be driving ahead of the race and needed to get a head start on them.

I then walked to the team paddock. I managed to get to the INEOS bus and had a lovely chat with Rod. It was scorching hot today. Rod and I leant up against the INEOS bus trying to catch some shade. Still hot there though. Some of the riders were by then riding off to sign on. I took a great picture of Alaphilippe riding along the path. And one of Simon Geschke. The Lidl Trek bus had baskets of fresh fruit at their bus.

It was then a case of rushing back to the village for the loo before getting in the car and driving off along the route. We drove past several of the tour sponsors personnel dressed up in random costumes. A giant orange cone which I assume was meant to be a volcano. A man made up to look like he was made of granite. They must have been melting in there.

We finally joined the race route just after the start line and drove off between the barriers lining the start. So cool to see all the fans lined out along the barriers from the inside! We eventually went through the sign depicting the 'Depart Real,' Kilometre Zero. I tried to take as many photos as I could through the car window of the people lining the route with the flags and hundreds of sunshades. There was hardly a gap between all the spectators along the entire route. Some of the campervans had so many flags on them and there were even some people in small tents. One campervan from Brittain had a replica Medieval Shield leaning against it.

Leclerc, the sponsor of the Polka dot jersey had been out early today as hundreds of people were wearing the polka dot t-shirts the give out by the thousand.

We were in a long line of other teams' cars, all driving pretty fast along the lovely smooth road. The route wound round the outside of the Puy de Dome, crossing yesterday's route just below the place where the roads closed on the stage finish there. I took a halfway decent picture of it too.

The views out of the window of the national park were amazing. We drove through some picturesque villages, mostly built of the local granite. I took a picture of a whole cliff of a volcanic formation of hexagonal granite pillars.

Next up was the first of the five climbs, a Cat 3, then a Cat 2 climb where I spotted Ruth and Matt sat at the top. I also spotted Jamie somewhere too. We drove over the only cat 2 climb and through the Sprint point before we stopped in a small town. We were about 75 kilometres into the race by then. Two other Jayco cars and one of their vans also stopped here so I got to meet lots more people. The town was pretty, with flowers everywhere.

The drive continued up and down hills, and through many pretty villages along smooth, wide roads, and smaller, twisty roads, to a point about 108 kilometres into the race. John and Vaz had provided filled baguettes for lunch which we ate as John drove along.

John and Vaz had been tasked with giving out bottles and bags at the 108 kilometre point but finding the exact conditions for this is quite tricky. A slight incline is preferable to a flat or downhill section. Slows the riders down. It needs to be quite straight and not on a bend, so the riders have time to spot them and get into position to take the bottle or bag. The

DS's must find out what the riders require and relay the info to John and Vaz so they can have the correct stuff ready. And of course, the car must be completely off the race route.

Once John had found exactly what he wanted I had a bit of time before the race arrived to check out some of the scenery and to find where I wanted to stand so I could film the race coming past and them giving out the bottles and bags. A few other teams had dropped people off in the same area, so it was fun.

A huge butterfly landed on my leg. It was so pretty. I transferred it to my hand so Vaz could film it properly. It was all white with small black spots around the edges and two 'tails' on the wings. Lovely.

Luke Durbridge (Jayco Alula), the DS and John got their wires crossed. It meant the riders wanted single bottles of water, but the DS had requested three bottles in a bag. I have the mess up on film. John got nothing away that time, but Vaz, a few metres further along the road, got his bottles collected successfully. John got his bottles and a bag away in the next groups on the road, so it was all good.

Back quickly to the car, join the race route in front of the grupetto, catch up to the riders ahead and then exit the race route as soon as we could to try and get to the finish before the race arrived there. John drove along these narrow, twisty roads so fast! We made it to the finish area with enough time for me to jump out and run to the race route before the riders came past. Such a brilliant day.

Just to mention, John had forgotten to fill the car up before the race. By the time we left the finish, joined the autoroute back to Clermont Ferrand, the gauge said we were empty! Vaz said John would be fine as he was always lucky like that. We made it to the petrol station on the autoroute so Vaz was right!

128

Thursday, 11th July 2019. Les Planche des Belle Filles.

My plan for the stage up to Les Planche les Belle Filles and the stage preceding it, were easy to work out this time. I knew I wanted to attempt to cycle up the final climb which would be the second time I had done this one. The finish had been extended by just over a kilometre to include a 24% gradient gravel section at the top. See the Stage 5 start in St Die des Vosges, then drive to near Belfort ready for Les Planche les Belle Filles the next day.

In St Die, I messaged George (team INEOS) to see if they had any spare entry passes today. The start was noticeably quiet with few fans about so I thought I would try my luck! 10 minutes later and I had my pass. Thanks George.

I was happily just standing beside the INEOS Bus watching the riders come past when George comes up and says – You know you were going to cycle up Les Planche des Belle Filles tomorrow? How would you like to go in a Helicopter over the race instead? That is the easiest question I have ever had to answer! I thought I had mis-heard him at first, but he was serious! Eventually I said just tell me where to be when and I would be there. No idea what happened for the rest of the day after that. Good job I wrote some of it down when I got to the next place I was staying as I still do not really remember it very clearly even now.

As I drove to the next place I am staying, I went right past Mulhouse where the start is for Stage 6. That meant I knew exactly how to get back in the morning and how long it would take which helped. The place I was staying was another Gite and it was lovely. I was in a small cottage attached to their house with its own entrance and its own car park. The host spoke fairly good English and was really nice. There was a lounge with a two piece suite, a dining table and a fully fitted kitchen. It even had a proper coffee machine with Senseo coffee. The Bedroom was separate with an en suite shower room. Lovely place to stay and cheap. 106 Euros for 2 nights including Breakfast!

I checked my e-mails and there was the invite for stage 6. Amazing. I had to do the usual update to get it added to my phone but that's easy. Next though I found I also had a parking permit to park in the centre in the VIP area, but that needed to be printed and I had no way of doing that at 8 at night. The Host had a printer and did it for me. So helpful and so kind. I love staying in Gites and small places in France. They are just the best.

I used my emergency rations again that night as I just could not be bothered to get anything else. I was way too excited! And I had eaten quite a lot during the day in the Village. Naturally sleeping that night was hard what with the coffee, and the excitement.

I was up early, dressed, and ready to go by 7 which is the time I had requested breakfast. The host duly knocked on the door at dead on 7 with a huge tray of food which he left on the dining table. It was amazing. Scrambled eggs, pancakes, bread, croissants, pain au chocolate, freshly made fruit smoothie, ham, cheese, enough for several people, not just me! It was tasty, and I managed to eat quite a lot of it. As for the plans for the day, I knew I would be going in a Helicopter, but I had no details at all as to what that entailed. I have kept the ticket though.

I left for Mulhouse at 8 as I had to be there by 10. It is only a 45 min drive, but I had no idea what to expect or where to go. But it was easy with my permit on display. I was guided right to the side of the race start. I got into the village at 10 and eventually found where I was supposed to be. It was only the ASO Hospitality box! I sat on a comfortable chair while they plied me with fruit, petit fours, more coffee, it was awesome. Christian Prudhomme was also in the box although not for long. There were two other people who were guests of Team INEOS and they arrived shortly after I did. It was Helen Standen and her husband. She is on Twitter as INEOS Ted as she makes all sorts of jumpers for a bunch of teddies. I have messaged her before. We were then introduced to our host for the day, Jeremy. He is an ex pro rider who rode the Tour de France a few times, the last in 2011. He also rode the tour of Britain in 2012 but broke his collar bone on the last stage so had to miss representing France in the Worlds.

We were given proper passes on a lanyard. We left the village and headed into the Paddock d'Equipes. I had a fun time in there. I managed to get a selfie with Alberto Contador! And another with Eric Zabel, who won the green jersey five times! Also, Alex Dowsett, Nicholas Roche, loads of people. I also got a proper French greeting from Ashley House! And chatted with Daniel Friebe for about 10 mins.

Jeremy said it was time to go then and he took us right up to the sign on podium. We were standing right by the ramp where all the riders rode up to sign on. It was brilliant! I took loads of pictures of practically everyone. That was amazing. So close I could hear the bikes on the surprisingly steep ramp as they all rode up.

Next, Jeremy finally said it was time to go again and we started to walk along the route to the start area which is off limits to everyone. We just walked straight through. Geraint Thomas was cycling along towards the depart point and he stopped so we could have our photo taken with him by our own personal photographer. Never did catch his name but he is going to send out the pictures later.

We walked down right beside the riders lining up at the start, through the start line and into an official race car. It was green and covered in Skoda stickers. We were going to drive along the race route ahead of the race for a while, through the 'depart real' and on to a good place to stop and wait for the race to catch us up. I took loads of photos and videos of all the people on the side of the road.

As an ex cyclist (which all the official sponsored car drivers are apparently) Jeremy was an amazing driver. And we had to go fast as we had to stay in front of the peloton. It is amazing how fast this race is going. On one of the downhill sections later Jeremy drove as fast as the riders would go! Scary!

We could hear race radio as well with all the updates given by the ASO commentator in many different languages. He would say whatever was needed in whatever language the team impacted needed to hear it. Amazing. He also gave out updates of what was happening in the race in both French and English, so we knew who was in the break, how far ahead they were, where they were, what was coming up, everything.

Jeremy stopped the car at a point where he could take a turning to leave the race route, cut across country and re-join further along ahead of the race again. We watched as the race came past, but I just watched rather than film. I did speak to a local man there who told me all about the winery opposite. He did not speak English, but I got the gist of what he was saying which was good. We then got back in the car and drove off through some amazing scenery in the Vosges mountains. Lots of the teams' cars were doing the same thing as they were getting to the feed stations.

We re-joined the race route and drove up and over two of the early cols. We also followed the Team INEOS car that Xabi was in, up one of the many hills. Then about 1.30 we stopped for lunch! That was all laid out under a huge cover with tables and chairs, and free glasses of Champagne. There was also a glass of local red wine on offer, which naturally would have been rude to refuse! The food was individually prepared for each person with extra nibble bits and some more fruit available as well. Plus, Cola, lemonade, and water.

At this point, the Helicopters arrived and parked up in a field next to the route. There are five of them and mine was going to be number 2! It is an amazing sight. Our pilot was called Teo. We were near the mid-point of the penultimate climb at that point, so we got to see the race come past again. Andre Greipel was still just about in touch with the day's breakaway, which was an astonishing ride by him as a huge Sprinter. Movistar were really going for it at the front of the peloton at that point too.

We stayed and watched the rest of the riders come past then went out to the helicopter. I sat in the front with a glass floor under my feet so I could look down on the race below. We took off second of the five and flew round and round over the race below us for about 30 minutes! Up the penultimate climb, down the other side and along a short valley. What a view, what an experience! What fun! I took videos, and photos but mostly just looked out of the helicopter at the stunning scenery and the race lined out below. You could see all the peloton and the race infrastructure, and from there you could also get a sense of just how steep the climbs were as you could see all of it. The TV helicopter was below us. The crowds were massive. The helicopter was quite high up, but everything was just fantastic. I have no idea how I am ever going to top that for an experience!

The helicopters all landed on a football pitch on the downhill part of the penultimate climb. Jeremy was waiting for us in the car and drove us the rest of the way along the race route and up the final climb. Such amazing scenes with all the thousands of fans all over the mountain. We parked up just off the race route at a point with 1 kilometre to go and we were then escorted into one of the giant four storey hospitality boxes/houses for more food and more champagne on the roof terrace overlooking the race route. And we could see the big screen on the opposite side of the race route as well. What a view! Andy Schleck (ex pro rider who I saw in Mondorf les Bains a few years ago) was there and I got a great selfie with him. He stayed to chat about Yorkshire with me.

The race came past, and it was an awesome finale. How Alaphilippe managed to nearly beat Geraint Thomas up that mountain, and did beat many of the other GC guys, was brilliant. And another newbie in the Yellow Jersey. Magic. The view from the balcony was great looking down on the race as it passed. I could see everything. The riders, the cars, the motor bikes, the fans, everything. I loved it.

Eventually it was time to say goodbye to Jeremy, but I will see him again in the Village Depart on another stage start somewhere. As we were leaving, we were given a parting gift of these awesome bags. Cannot just call them bags though. They were more like holdalls made of Canvas and Leather the same volume as my small, wheeled suitcase. There was a smaller canvas and leather wash bag inside. These bags were also full of food and drinks. We were then escorted to a coach to be transferred off the mountain and back to Mulhouse. More food, more drink on board but I had no alcohol this time. I did have to drive! Getting off the mountain took ages as everything, and everybody must go down the same road. We left the race at 6.10 but did not get back to Mulhouse until gone 9 pm and technically on any other day it would only take 45 minutes. The road that the bus had to take was not the road the race had come up. That was reserved for the riders and the team cars only. We had to take this small logging track that wound all over the mountain. In a giant bus!

We then went on towards Belfort which was the start for the next day and where we should have been able to join the motorway back to Mulhouse, but the road to that had already been closed so the driver had to wind all over the place to get to the next junction about 10 miles away.

The bus only dropped me off right next to my car! What a day. What an experience. How lucky am I?! I was back at the Gite by 10 though and still buzzing.

George messaged me to ask if I enjoyed my day. It was way beyond that. I just have no idea how to begin to thank him for this experience. But I did try!! I also got loads of messages from the Lasses when I finally managed to update on their Facebook page!

Would I recommend one of the VIP trips to anyone? YES! They are extremely expensive but if you can afford it, then do it!

The more people you are able to interact with, the more chance of getting treats. Just don't ask for them or expect them.

10

Intermediate Sprint Points

Tuesday, 29th June 2021. Vitre.

Today was stage 4 of this year's tour and I had stayed in the same place for the last four nights as I could get to points of all the first three stages from there. Today I had to move to a new location, so it was going to be a transition day for me to get me to Change for the ITT the next day. A three or four hour drive in total so the best option for today was to go to the intermediate Sprint point in Vitre. The last day in this lovely B&B. Breakfast was even better today as the host made me two soft boiled eggs! And some excellent fresh ground coffee. And orange juice, croissants, so much food. I was in no hurry this morning either which was nice. I had arranged to pick Emma up just after 10 so a very restful start to the day.

Vitre is an incredibly old town with a Cathedral and a Castle, and only two or three hours from the B&B depending on traffic. I had the parking place identified already and parked exactly where I intended to. It was just 10 kilometres from the autoroute so nice and easy. We were parked by 12 so we had loads of time to look around before the race arrived about 3.30.

What a beautiful place. It had a stunning Cathedral at one end of the main street which was going to be the race route with the sprint point just in front of it. We had a wander all-round the outside of that with its plazas and old buildings. It was an extremely hot day again, so we stopped at a small café on the square by the cathedral and I had a rum and raisin milk shake with whipped cream. Lovely.

From there we walked down some seriously old and narrow streets. The houses along these streets were so old, and some were definitely Wonky! I took loads of pictures of the side streets, the strange, shaped houses, and the wonky buildings. The whole place was amazing.

From there we found the castle. Again, great photo opportunity as it was quite pretty. Not Albi standard but still lovely. The houses were more interesting to me as I have no idea how some of them were still standing. One had this first floor room that stuck out from the rest of the house! I love old, wonky, strange buildings. It looked a wonderful place for a ghost walk!

So, back to the race. Emma wanted to see the riders come past with the Cathedral as back drop for her photos. Have I mentioned she is a Photographer? As you are aware, I am not! I wanted to watch them come sprinting up the 3% slope to the sprint point. I found a perfect place to watch from. I was at 50 metres to go on the outside of a slight curve in the road. I could see for 100 metres in both directions and right through the finish line.

The crowds were quite light so only 2 or 3 deep all the way along both sides of the road. There was also a high kerb to the side of the road with the barriers on the road below it, so I had an excellent view. Being on the outside of the bend also meant that I could see the race when it came through as the riders would be on the inside of the bend. Perfect.

When the race came past, I was able to watch the full Quick Step lead out train in action right up to Morkov dropping Cav off with 50 metres to go for the win and 30 Green jersey points. It was a perfect lead out and a textbook sprint. And so fast! I managed to get the whole thing on video too without looking at the screen. This was much more fun than a sprint finish. Less crowds, less pushing, less stress, also less speed but you cannot have everything!

Saturday, 15th July 2017. Rabastens.

After two days of cycling up mountains, I slept like I had been knocked out that night. I woke up a bit stiff the following morning which was no surprise at all. I had a long drive that day as well, approximately 500 kilometres, but I had split that into two sections for the day. I tried some stretches early on before being sat still in the car all day which helped a bit, but I could really have done with a massage.

I left the Pyrenees about 9 in the morning for the first leg of my journey. This was 200 kilometres to the Intermediate Sprint point of the day at a place called Rabastens. It was a nice and easy place to get to and still stay on the right side of the race route to avoid all road closures. In fact, all I had to do was drop off the Autoroute and drive for just 3 kilometres to the edge of the town. And then park and walk a few hundred metres to the actual race route. The Intermediate Sprint point itself was just outside the town but still within easy walking distance.

I arrived at Rabastens just after 10.30 and found a suitable place to park. It was just off the road into town, down a large side road leading to some factory buildings and it had a long line of overhanging trees along one side with a wide grass verge under them. I left the car there in the shade and set off for the town to have a look round. They had a great market in full swing. One Spanish couple had a stall getting ready to cook a huge Paella which looked delicious. There was one stall that only sold cheeses. Unfortunately, I had no fridge so could not buy any of that although I did sample some of them. There was another stall dedicated solely to local bread products which smelt just so tasty as I walked past. Another stall had lots of cooked meats like salamis and ham etc. There was even a stall just for Olives! The whole place was buzzing.

The race was due to come through at 2.30 ish so I had plenty of time to look around the town which was bigger than I thought it would be. Eventually I stopped for a coffee in one of the cafes along the main street which again unfortunately, was barely drinkable but meant I could sit down for a while and just watch people going past. It was also hot again, around 30 to 32 degrees and the café had a nice, shaded patio in front of it which was surprisingly cool.

The town itself had a main road running right through it that had two right angle bends, first right and then left, just after the road entered the town and just past the Intermediate Sprint point. I decided that the best place to watch would be between the two bends as that would string the race out into one lengthy line of riders.

I bought the Paella to take away. It was only seven euros, and I got a huge portion with six large Prawns and a huge Chicken leg! It was rice based not bread based so it was great. I then wandered towards the sprint point and found a tree to lean against on a grass verge, blew up one of the Ibis Cushions, and sat on it by the side of the road eating paella which was tasty and filling. The Ibis Cushions are some of the tat that is thrown from the caravan each time and I try and collect as many of these as I can as they are extremely useful even if they do not last very long. I do not think they are meant to be sat on!

Eventually it was getting towards time for the race to arrive. All the walking I had done had loosened my stiffness up no end by then, so I was able to stand at the side of the road under my Brolly and wait for the race with no issues. I got another wave from Rod as he went past in the car. He cannot really miss me with a pink brolly up! When the race came past it was all strung out in a single line as I had hoped, and I managed to take a halfway decent video of this. The front riders swept round then you could see the following riders all sprinting just to hold the wheel in front. I think at least one commentator has described this action as like a piece of elastic being stretched out and then trying to close back up again and that is exactly what it is like. You just cannot get the full experience of this effect from the TV pictures. It does not matter where you watch the race go past, there is always something new to see or to discover or to experience.

All the cars and motorbikes (and there are lots and lots of them) all came past next. Finally, the broom wagon came and went, and it was all gone. Less than 5 minutes start to finish. It is still well worth a visit to see them all whizz past though. That was me done here as I had to head off to get to the next hotel in Le Puy en Velay which was still 300 kilometres away. I had to get around Rodez which was where that day's stage was due to finish, and I had no idea what roads were going to be closed. There was no other way I could go that avoided Rodez though.

Heading back towards my car, I finally spotted one of the Green Tour directions arrows that I could get at. These are prized souvenirs, and you will see loads of them in every campervan that you pass. I had to climb up a lamp post in front of a table full French people enjoying an afternoon drink in the sun. That got quite a laugh from them, but I finally have my first Green Arrow and I have been after one since the first day I arrived. And I did not need my scissors as this one was attached by twisted cable ties.

My car was not too hot when I got back, and I had a short drive to get on the Autoroute. As I was nearing Rodez, I saw the Caravan going passed on the road next door. However, I managed to get all the way round Rodez with no problems which was great. I then had to head across towards Mende via the A75. Fortunately, I was going to be following the road towards Mende which meant I turned North on to the A75 and not South as that led towards the Millau Viaduct! I went over another viaduct off the A75 instead and that was bad enough! The side winds on that were SCARY!!!! I would have driven under the Millau Viaduct if I could but there is no way I am driving over it! Check it out on Google as its worth a look. The scenery however was breath taking all the way from Rodez to Mende and then from Mende to Le Puy en Velay it turned spectacular with volcanic structures all over the place. I am still sounding like a French travel agent but because I am led round France by the Tour route, I get to see so much that I had no idea even existed.

My first view of Le Puy en Velay was also spectacular. The town centre is built on a volcanic plug with a Cathedral perched on the top and surrounded by small streets and alleyways of beautiful buildings. All the streets and alleyways are paved with Flint or Cobbles and the whole effect is just lovely. I arrived just before 7.30 that evening and found the Chambre d'Hotes easily. It was just a large house set well back from a narrow side street. It had its own underground car park. I was able to lock my car in here with plenty of room to put my bike out as well and do some essential maintenance on it. The room I was staying in was huge. And the adjoining bathroom was the same size again. The owner is just lovely but with limited English. My French must be improving slightly as we were able to converse quite well.

Tuesday, 9th July 2018. Derval.

A slightly more leisurely day today! I left the Gite at around 9.30 this morning. That was a lovely place to stay, and I really felt very at home there. The owners were just lovely even if they did not speak any English.

I drove to Derval which is a small village just south of Rennes. I managed to park the car right under a tree which was perfect as it is a scorcher again today. Topped out around 32 degrees. It did cloud over about 3 so cooled down to about 29 then.

I walked into the centre of the village, and it was a hive of activity. They had built a temporary tent type village outside the church just off the race route. They had tour souvenir stalls, some bars, lots of food places and a children's bike park where they were letting kids ride over wooden obstacles. There was a stage set up for live music later and a band was warming up when I arrived.

The tour had unfolded one of its many portable TV screens in front of the church. These are transported in lorries which have a sliding roof panel through which the giant TV screen is raised. Once they are done in that location, the TV screen is lowered back down again and driven to the next place it is to be used.

The church had a small plaza next to it with a road running outside that. Everything was set up along both sides of this road and all over the plaza. The towns people were obviously planning a bit of a parade along this road at some point as a whole bunch of Samba Dancers and drummers all dressed up in great costumes with masses of long feathers and waving Brazilian flags were massing ready to set off. They look amazing. So much colour, so pretty and the Samba rhythms they were playing were great.

I wandered round looking at what was going on for a while. Then I walked the 2 kilometres to the actual sprint point which was outside the village. In a car park outside the local supermarket on the edge of the village there were around 50 campervans parked. They were having a sort of street party along the shady side of the street. There were loads of them, mostly French. I spoke to a Father and his two sons nearer the sprint point who were from Portsmouth. The father had driven from St Malo and the two sons had cycled. They have a holiday home about 5 kilometres north of Derval.

I took a few photos of a deserted sprint point (will be packed later) and then walked back to find a good place in the town to sit and wait. It had to be on the shady side as it was just too hot even under the brolly.

I took some pictures of the madness that is the caravan and posted them on the Yorkshire Lasses Facebook page as today's offering of my tour update. It really is insane. Anyway, the race came flashing past and that was it. I made use of the large supermarket before I left to stock up on food to cook that evening as I was staying in my own little bungalow near Mur-de-Bretagne.

Hints and tips.

Are sprint points worth a visit? Yes, but only if you cannot find anything better to do. The places are usually very pretty and often have something going on in the centre.

The actual sprint point is frequently outside the town or village and often quite boring to be honest.

The sprint is much slower, and less contentious and just less really. I was lucky with the sprint in Vitre which was the exception rather than the rule.

Again, make sure you are on the correct side of the race route to travel wherever you are going next as the route will still be closed for ages after the race has passed.

Trains could be possible but unlikely as most of the places are small.

Miscellaneous

This chapter is to cover anything I could not find a separate category for, and there are lots of these, but I have just picked some random ones.

Tuesday, 11th July 2017. Périgueux to Bergerac.

Today's stage was an unusual one. The start in Périgueux was only 50 kilometres from the finish in Bergerac but the race route went round in a giant horseshoe shape for 178 kilometres. In my car, it would only take me 30 minutes to get from the start to the finish while the riders took 5 hours plus. I had also decided to watch the finish from about 5 kilometres from the end as I had not done that before and the road there looked like it should provide a great place to watch. A sprint finish did not interest me, especially when there is something else to experience.

My day started with a great breakfast again, then I loaded up the car and left it in the car park at the hotel. They were quite happy to let me leave it there for the entire day. I then headed off to the start area and had a good look round as the start was not until 13.10. The layout today was that the team buses would park either side of a dual carriage way that had a large grassed central reservation running down the middle of it. The barriers had been erected down both edges of the dual carriage way keeping the crowd on the path on either side. When the caravan came down just one side of the carriageway it distracted the security guys who watched the caravan instead of the barriers. You can get into the barriered area with a pass but as he was not looking, I just walked in! I mixed with the photographers and tried to look as if I should be there, and it worked! At least, I did not get thrown out.

The buses then arrived and parked on both carriageways, and I was able to stay there all the time. That meant I got some fabulous pictures. I was able to speak to Rod again and he is still interested in everything I am doing and seeing at the Tour which means such a lot to me. He deals with the logistics of moving everything around France for Team Sky and with who goes where and does what regarding driving and handing out bottles and food in various places on route. All of which I find fascinating. He does loads of other stuff too, but we only had about 5 minutes to talk today.

I got some good pictures of Froome, and all the team sky guys, even one of Sergio Henao's badly scared legs from all the operations he needed after an horrific crash. I finally have an excellent picture of Contador or at least I like it. It is the first time I have managed to get a photo of any kind that has Contador in it. I got pictures of loads of other riders quite close up.

I was able to walk along easily to every bus this time and see anyone I wanted to. I went over to the Orica Scott bus as I had been watching their backstage pass video diaries and the whole team seemed to just have loads of fun all the time. I went to the BMC bus but that was a bit subdued following Porte's dreadful crash. At the Quick Step bus, Dan Martin could be seen moving very gingerly as he had hurt himself in Porte's crash. The shear fun of being in the VIP area reserved for accredited people (photographers, ASO guys, Gendarmes etc.) and invited guests (those there just for that one stage) and dodging all security guys was brilliant! (Unfortunately, Security had increased in the 2018 Tour and getting in without a pass is almost impossible now). Once the riders had moved off to the start I went back to my car and prepared to drive to the finish town of Bergerac.

As Périgueux town centre was closed to traffic until at least 4 pm my plan was to leave the Hotel car park in the wrong direction, go across the second road bridge over the river and take a back road in the general direction of the N21 to Bergerac if I could find it. What could go wrong with that plan? Nothing went wrong. I kept my sense of direction and found the road easily. It only took 35 minutes to get to Bergerac.

However, the plan for this place was extremely complicated as the race route went along the main N21, three-quarters of the way round the outside of the town itself cutting the whole place off effectively. And naturally, that road was closed.

My rough plan was to try and go through the west of the town and get out the other side, cross the river somewhere, then wriggle cross country towards the Airport as I knew the race would be running along one side of it. I needed to be south of the race route, so I could get to the next town where I was staying without getting caught up in the closed roads.

Wriggling through the town was not easy but I did manage it without any U-turns although the route I took did look a bit like a sidewinder snake trail. I found a suitable place to leave the car in a sort of closed layby or cul-de-sac and because I had my bike with me, I was able to sit and have lunch in the car before heading out to the race. Everyone else was walking.

The road was closed about 3 kilometres from the route so again, having a bike enabled me to see so much more. It only took me about 10 minutes to get to the race route and it also meant I could keep going until I found the best spot from which to watch the race.

The road from my car to the race route was a giant four lane dead straight road heading slightly up hill (the N21). It ran directly towards the Airport. At the end of this road was a roundabout and then a junction onto another giant four lane dead straight stretch of road (still the N21) going slightly downhill which ran alongside the Airport perimeter for at least 3 kilometres. This was the race route road. I cycled to just passed the junction and a little way down this road to where I had a tremendous view down the whole road that the race was due to come up. I spent some time talking to a father and son from England while we waited for the race to arrive. They were amazed by the caravan when it came past as it was their first time at the race. I managed to avoid all the tat today and left that to everyone else.

I got another wave from Rod as he drove past ahead of the race today. I was easy to spot as I was jumping up and down and waving my Brolly!

Wow! What a spectacular experience that was when the race came past here. I had no idea what to expect but it was amazing. The Breakaway was caught as the race turned the corner

3 kilometres down the straight and the whole peloton started to race up the slight incline towards me. The peloton was all lined out across the whole four lanes of the road in team order. There was no wind today, so the front of the peloton was flat.

The sprinters teams were represented with their giant lead out men. The GC teams were there and protected by their giant workhorses. And they were going so fast. The peloton riding directly towards you at full chat is a stunning sensory experience. There is the sight of them all lined out across the road. The colours, the size, the effort on the faces of the leading riders.

There is the noise as they get nearer, shouting, wheels on tarmac, bikes 'tinging' as wheels get too close together. There is also the 'feel' of what can only be described as a 'bow wave' of pressure as the bigger riders physically push the air out of their way and to the sides of the peloton. It is like an enormous lorry going past if you are standing at the side of the road.

There is also a strange sense of electricity or power emanating from the whole peloton. I have no idea how to explain that, but it is there. It is like an aura floating above the peloton. I guess it is a visual effect of the air being pushed up and over the peloton, but it is very visible. You can see the power being generated by the lead out men written all over their faces!

There is no other way to experience this than to go out to the Tour, stand on the side of the road, and see it for yourself. I would recommend this to anyone. There is no sense of any of this just watching it on TV.

I have been lucky enough to experience this on two separate occasions at the tour. It was by far the most amazing sensory experience of the race passing that I have ever had. The pre-requisites of experiencing this are –

1) Find a long straight stretch of road, between 6 and 3 kilometres from the finish. The longer the straight, the better the experience.
2) The road needs to be as wide as possible. The wider the road, the better the experience.

149

3) It must be an expected bunch sprint finish.
4) The wind needs to be light to non-existent.
5) The breakaway must be caught before they reach the beginning of the straight.

As you can see, it is not a given even if you find the correct place! But if all the points align you will not be disappointed. I look for these prerequisites on every planning session I do for each tour as I want to experience this again and again.

Monday, 3rd July 2023 Amorebieta-Etxano to Bayonne.

I do not get the opportunity to do this very often but today my plan was to see the start, then drive on the Autoroute towards France and stop at a point to watch the race come past at the top of a small climb. I was staying in a place at the foot of an entry ramp onto the autoroute, so leaving the start town was going to be easy. I then had at least 3 hours to get to the climb which would only take about 50 minutes of driving.

I had been staying in the most excellent B&B on the outskirts of Amorebieta-Etxano which is about 30 kilometres from Bilbao. I had been able to get to the 'Grand Depart' in the centre of Bilbao, to the top of a final climb back into the finish in Bilbao and to a downhill in a national park about 50 kilometres away for stage 2. Today, the start was right outside my door!

After another excellent breakfast which included a poached egg and some crispy bacon, I loaded up my car which I was able to leave in their secure car park. I then walked 200 metres along the actual race route to the start line. If I turned left out of the B&Bs small access road onto the main roundabout, I would be able to drive up to the autoroute easily as the race route was going right at that roundabout.

The sign on podium was in a huge carpark to one side of the start line so I wandered up to that first. It was a bit early, so it was still being constructed. Behind the podium was a big park running alongside the river with several paths which made it easy to walk behind the podium and on towards the town for everything else. The whole of the main road through the centre of the town was lined with barriers as the roll out was due to go north through here, then round in a circle back to the roundabout I was staying near in the south.

I was heading along this path towards the town centre when I met Marc Chauvet, the voice of the tour at every start. I have spoken to him before, and we had a lovely chat again today. Everything is very relaxed this early in the morning before a start. In fact, everything was very relaxed, unlike the start in Bilbao! That had been manic!

The village depart was set up next on my walk along the riverside. That had taken over a second carpark between the river and the main road. I had no entry ticket today unfortunately as I would love to have tried some of the local Spanish delicacies.

The Paddock d'Equipes was next and was just a long narrow road running parallel to the main road. That was also already barriered off. No way was this going to be big enough for all the teams to fit in it.

At the end of this by a bridge, a huge stage was being erected. It had massive speakers all over it, so I assumed it was for a live band or concert later.

I walked round the end of the Paddock, and then turned towards the race roll out route. I was still looking for the Fan Park. I walked all the way back along the main road, looking into every side street but I never found it. No Idea where it was. There is always a Fan Park somewhere. This meant no Senseo Coffee. Disaster! Little was open in the town, but I eventually found a place selling coffee back near the Paddock.

I waited until the caravan had left before heading to see how the buses were getting on squeezing into the paddock. Because of the small roads, they had all had to wait until the caravan had passed through and out of the town before they could come in. Some of the corners were a bit tight too, but the drivers are amazing.

All but four teams made it into the paddock. IPT, Jayco, Total energies and Jumbo did not. The INEOS bus was about four teams along, inside the barriers. That did mean I could have a lovely chat with Gary at the IPT bus today. John Trevorrow was at the Jayco bus, and I got a lovely hug from him.

I could also chat to Rod, Steve Cummings, Ian Stannard and Hannah at the INEOS bus.

It was difficult to wander up and down outside the barriers as the gap was very narrow, so I stayed near the INEOS bus and watched the riders all come past. I have so many photos from today! Peter Sagan, what a great picture that is. An Excellent one of Tom Pidcock. The one of Mat Hayman is lovely even though he was wearing a mask. I was also wearing a mask as Rod have given me a few more of the INEOS masks. I took a selfie with Ian Stannard as we had matching masks which looks so funny!

Ben O'Conner stopped for a chat with Rod right next to me. That is also a great picture. Wout van Aert went past too but he was wearing a mask the covered his almost his whole face!

I got a picture of a Yates twin in the Jayco kit and I know which one it is. Simon, as Adam was riding for UAE. The picture of Simon and Luke Durbridge is excellent, in focus and right in the middle of the shot. I am still not a photographer though so lots of other pictures were fuzzy and off centre.

Once the riders had all cycled off to the start, I nipped through a short alley way to try and film the roll out through the town centre but that was packed. So many people. I watched the heads of the riders all go past and the film was ruined by a giant of a man with a bald head!

From there I practically ran back to my car and drove straight up onto the A8 towards France within 30 minutes of the race leaving. It was then just a 30 minute drive to the point I had identified to watch the race come past again. The race route wriggled its way along small roads towards the finish in Bayonne in France but crossed the A8 right by a service station. I turned into the service station and parked in the car park there which left me with an 800 metre walk to the race route at the KOM for the top of the Cat 3 climb near Itziar. It was so easy. Such a rare opportunity for the race route to enable this.

The race was expected about 50 minutes after I had arrived. I found a wonderful place to wait, just before the KOM banner, behind the barriers with a view straight down the hill for about 500 metres.

The two breakaway riders came across first and the rest of the peloton a couple of minutes later. The view was perfect and both videos came out well too.

I was in my hotel in Dax by 5 so a great end to an enjoyable day. I could do with a bowl of hot water for my poor feet though!

Saturday, 26th June 2021. La Course for Women and Men's Stage 1 – Brest to Landerneau.

The ladies' race was supposed to be over this course but on the Sunday, the day after the mens stage 1 but ASO had changed it in the last few days to be on the same day, just incredibly early. The ladies' race had also been changed to a shorter section of the mens route with the finish as a circuit race of four laps round the centre of Landerneau.

My plan for today was therefore quite complicated but I thought it should be possible. First, the ladies race. The best option was to watch them four times on the circuit somewhere in the centre of Landerneau. Where I would watch from was dependent on being able to get back to the Mens race route near the bridge on the N165 for Kilometre Zero. I would then try and get back into Landerneau for the finish of the mens race somewhere on the final hill hopefully.

Planning was important here to get the most from a very unusual day. Access to the D29 between Landerneau and the N165 over the Pont Albert Louppe as the race exit from Brest was critical to my plan. The race route dropped off the N165 just after the bridge so I hoped I would be able to get far enough along the N165 to reach a point where I could access the D29. After Kilometre Zero, my plan was to then drive back along the D29 into Landerneau, park by the roundabout again and then walk the 3 kilometres to anywhere I could get on the final climb to the finish. It should work!

I had breakfast in the excellent B&B I was booked in for 3 nights. It was lovely! Fruit, Cereals, milk, croissants, pain au chocolat, bread, honey, jams, percolated coffee, cake, and yogurt! And all included in the price. I needed to leave quite early this morning as I wanted to watch the Ladies race which would come through Landerneau 4 times before 11.15. It took just over an hour to get to where I hoped the road into Brest would close so I could follow my plan A route from the main road. And I was right! The road closed at the roundabout before the one for the D29, but I knew I could get there on a small back road.

I made it to the D29 and drove into Landerneau stopping when I reached the Roundabout on the junction with the race route. I parked right before this roundabout. That meant I would only have 20 metres to walk to start looking for somewhere to watch the Ladies race. I decided to walk to the bottom of the hill to the river and watch from the bridge so I could watch the descent, then the bridge and then up the hill on the other side. Four times. The final lap, I would be just 5 kilometres from the finish line.

I had 20 minutes to wait for them to come round the first time, which was not enough time to set my Yorkshire flag up on the bridge. The break of about five riders came past first with the peloton split into two groups already. Lizzie Deignan (she lives near me in Otley) was in the second group on the road. They were going so fast. Such power, such grace, such speed, I love watching the Ladies race. Unfortunately, few other people were watching which is a great shame. There were, however, more at the finish but still not enough.

After 2 passes, I decided to move up towards the roundabout so I could see more of the downhill part. Circuit races give you the option to change your mind. The view there was even better as I could appreciate the speed more.

After they came round the final time, I went back to the car and followed the D29 out towards the N165 as far as I could which was practically all the way. I just abandoned the car on the side of the road and walked the 100 metres to the race route. I found a long straight piece of road to watch from about 2 kilometres from Kilometre zero. The view I got of the race was fantastic. There were 5 or 6 riders trying to break away from the rest of the peloton who were all lined out in almost single file, and I could even identify individual riders just before they got to me. I managed to get the whole thing on video too, in the middle of the shot and just about in focus!

Back to the car then, drive back to the first place I had parked, then try and aim for the 2000 metres to go point. I tried walking towards the river in the town centre with the intention of turning right there onto the race route and walking up from there. The road was closed. To everyone. I am not surprised now I have seen it though as it was so narrow.

I retraced my route and took the first left turn I could, then the next left I came to as well. I kept on doing that on increasingly smaller roads until I finally came to one that was pointing towards the race route again. That led to a reasonable sized road and the race route at the 3000 metre point. I was 1 kilometre short of where I wanted to be but after a 5 kilometre walk instead of 2, I could go no further! ASO had placed some Port-a-loos on the junction which was helpful of them.

I managed to find a surprisingly good place against the barriers to watch the race come up the hill. I had about an hour to wait so I used my trusty picnic mat to sit on the kerb against the barriers while I waited.

Quite a few people were having proper parties on the opposite side of the road here. It was great fun to watch them although I suspect they had been drinking for a while as they were a bit worse for wear!

I had a view of the race route downhill from my vantage point for about 100 metres all the way to a level crossing. They even had a train come past! Good job it as on time. I could then see a bit of the road going uphill as well. The roadside was packed so I felt incredibly lucky to have found a spot beside the barriers.

I was right at the point that Alaphilippe attacked! He was going so fast with a whole bunch of riders chasing after him. It was awesome. Riders continued to come up that horribly steep hill for about 15 minutes. There had been several crashes on the stage today, (Omi, Opie placard day if you want to look it up!) and lots of riders were badly cut up.

Excellent first day for me though. And I had managed to miss the Caravan for the entire day. Result! I had plenty of stages to see that later.

Once the last rider had come past, I cut across in as direct line as I could back to my car. I ended up walking about 2.5 kilometres back to the car which was ok. The drive back to the B&B was easy and trouble free and meant I was in their lovely swimming pool by about 7 pm. That helped a great deal with getting my muscles working again.

Hints and tips.

Main one is Plan everything. The more you try and squeeze into a day, then the better your planning will need to be.

Do not get too close to the peloton. It will be going much faster than you expect.

Planning tips.

The next years route of the Tour de France is always announced with great fanfare by ASO (owners, and organisers of the tour) towards the end of October. The first three stages are always announced much earlier but that is not a great help if you have no idea where the rest of the tour will go and what it will entail. I usually wait until October before I decide my route.

I am retired and single, so I am lucky in that I can follow the entire three weeks of the tour round France and can select exactly what I want to do as soon as the route is announced. For a shorter visit, you will need a lot more details. The race timings would help a great deal for any planning when travelling by public transport, but that will not be available until May at the earliest.

Unfortunately, at this point, much of the actual route is guesswork. You will know which village, town, or city the race will start in but not exactly where within the town. There are sites shortly after the announcement that will detail the roads to be followed but only from Kilometre zero. This point can easily be several kilometres outside the start town. And the start time can range from 11 am to 2 pm!

If you decide that a start is what you want to see, there are options. If you cannot get anywhere to stay within the start town, then ASO have announced the setting up of bike parks at every start and finish. I would always recommend travelling with a bike even if you are not a cyclist. I am not a cyclist, but my bike has enabled me to get to see everything I want to.

Occasionally, in start towns that have a tram service, this is often free on the day of the tour. Also, a great help. Trains are useful too and cheap in France. Buses will be hit and miss due to all the road closures. Parking as close to the start as possible is an option but nothing is laid on for motorists by the tour. And road closures are not announced by the organisers. Local authorities do have some details online if you search for it but only from June onwards. Planning where to park can be tricky.

For finishes, you will have more details. The actual route will be available on online sites shortly after the announcement, which will show the roads used in any village, town, or city, and also roughly where the mountain top finishes will be.

You can get almost everything you will need for a sprint finish as they are normally in a town and will finish around the 5.30 pm mark. Again, there will be bike parks here which will help if you are driving. Or if the nearest train station is any distance away. Mountain stages with a flat or downhill run in are also usually in a town.

A summit finish will also aim to finish around the 5.30 mark but is likely to be in the middle of nowhere. There may even be only one road to access it from. Parking a car at the base of a climb is unlikely. You need to expect to leave your car several kilometres from the base of the climb. This needs a lot of planning as to how far you are prepared to either walk or cycle to get there. Buses are a possibility, but trains are very unlikely to be of any help here.

The rest of the stage routes can be found online showing the roads used to get from the start to the finish and some of the features of each stage. There will be no categories of mountains available, but you can get details of the length and the average gradient as well as the base and the summit locations. Again, no timings until May which is a shame as timing makes the planning so much easier.

If there are any cobbles or gravel stages, then the details of exactly where each sector is will start and finish is not be available without some detailed investigation using goggle earth. Some online sites give the profile of the stage with the sectors names and rough locations but matching the two together to get exact locations is complicated. And of course, there will be no timings available.

Transport to any of these sections by train or bus is non-existent. A vehicle will be required or a long cycle ride. Staying in the area close enough to walk to a sector is again unlikely as they are in very rural areas with few houses or villages.

I have never been able to identify a sprint point until ASO divulge this information in late May or early June.

How to plan what you can do for your trip to the tour, or for any bike race.

Step 1 – Decide how long you are going to go for, what dates, and how long it will take you to get to France. Also, once you know the route, does it have an airport, car hire, campervan hire, ferry, train station, anything you might need to get to the area. If you decide to travel round France by train, most of the train stations have facilities for leaving your luggage but you will need to book this in advance.

Step 2 – What do you want to experience? Place your selections in order of preference. For example, Mountain top finish, Start, then time trial. Whatever you feel will give you the most for however long you are able to go to the Tour for.

Step 3 – Check out the route in detail around the dates you have available. Look for long transfers, short transfers, same finish then start towns, mountains that are close to each other. Try and avoid days that have lots of the same thing such as four sprint stages in a row.

Step 4 – If you decide you can go for a full week for example, be ambitious in what you want to achieve but realistic also. The more planning you do beforehand, the more you will identify what is possible. If your week coincides with stages 8, 9, the rest day, 10, 11, 12 and 13 this will be a Saturday to Friday. You can expect a mountain of some sort in this but not necessarily a summit finish. There is unlikely to be a TT in this week. There could also be a huge transfer on the rest day. The longest I had to contend with was 700 kilometres!

Step 5 – Decide if you want to hire a car or drive your own if that is feasible. Do you want to hire a campervan? Can you manage on public transport? Do you have a bike? Is an electric bike a good option for you? Do you have your own bike or can you hire one? Then match the preferred method of travel to the route. Remember, Campervans are very limiting regarding travel options as to get to any stage you will either have to park and then travel or stay in one spot for most of the week. Gites are my favourite options for stays.

Step 6 – Book everything you need to on free cancellation if possible. The actual detailed route, the start town layouts, the race timings, the sprint points, the mountain classifications, the bike parking locations, and road closure information are not available until the end of May, or early June. They might mean you need to tweak your itinerary.

Step 7 – It is all very well getting to where you want to be, but you should also check out how to get away again afterwards. If you are driving, make sure you never have to cross the race route to get where you need to be next. The roads do not open quickly after the race has passed. They are sometimes still closed the next day! Also, official race vehicles have priority. Try and keep away from whichever way they are likely to go. If you are travelling by public transport, check the time of the last train or bus. You may be surprised at how early these can be.

Step 8 – Once you have your basic plan defined, then if you can, drill down into an almost hour by hour plan. That might sound a bit like overkill, but it is the only way to find out if you plan will work. The more days you do and the more stages you are going to see something of, then the more detailed your plan will need to be.

Other issues that need to be incorporated in your planning.

Mountains are often closed to everyone as the race arrival approaches. This is often 3 or 4 hours before the race is due. And is rigorously enforced! If you are cycling to the top, then leave plenty of time to get there. Fines are imposed if you are not careful. The Gendarmerie are not fond of allowing you to cycle back down afterwards sometimes, so look out for them.

If you are cycling down from a mountain summit finish, the riders will often also be cycling back down. They go extremely fast! They will be blowing whistles to warn you that they are coming past so get out of their way. They are unlikely to slow down.

The heat in France in July is intense. If you have a car or campervan, then trees are a godsend. Always try to find one to park under. Once, I could not find a place to park with any shade at all, and all the Haribo I had collected from the Publicity Caravan on previous days and left in my car, melted into gelatinous blobs!

It is wise to include where you are going to eat in your planning. France has a habit of closing early and not opening at all on Sundays. In rural France it is quite easy to get caught out.

Talk to people whenever and wherever you can. Dress up if you feel like it. Wear Lycra if you want to. It is a 3,500 kilometre party, so do whatever you want to. Just make sure you enjoy every minute.

The Tour route is different each year. You will be able to find hidden gems all over France that you would never have visited without the tour. Most holiday makers fly straight over these and only see resorts along the coast. France has so much more to offer.

Do not get in the riders' way. If you have any flares, leave them at home!! Seriously, they should not be anywhere near a bike race. If you have any random cardboard signs, then keep them OFF the race route! That goes for flags, selfie sticks, camaras, chairs, sunshades, dogs, children, cars, campervans, everything really! The OMI OPI lady who caused such a lot of damage to so many riders was lucky to get away as lightly as she did with just a healthy fine.

Watch the race itself as it passes, not through the viewfinder of your phone. You are there, not watching on television!

Wait until the Broom wagon has passed before leaving. Why go all that way and not watch everything?

All the above will apply to any other race as well – Spain or Italy's grand tours, the classics, one week races, but they are all far more relaxed! Except Paris - Roubaix obviously.

Most of all, go. Get there somehow. See something of the tour. It is an amazing experience.

Printed in the United States
by Baker & Taylor Publisher Services